Chapter 1: Introduction to the Lazy Webinar Method

Understanding Passive Income

Understanding passive income is essential for anyone looking to leverage the power of the Lazy Webinar method. Passive income refers to earnings derived from ventures in which a person is not actively involved. This concept is particularly appealing because it allows individuals to generate revenue with minimal ongoing effort after the initial setup. In the context of webinars, passive income can be achieved through automated systems that continually attract leads and convert them into sales, even while the creator focuses on other pursuits.

The primary appeal of passive income lies in its potential for financial freedom. By building automated webinar funnels, entrepreneurs can create a sustainable income stream without the need for constant active participation. Once a webinar is crafted, recorded, and integrated into a sales process, it can be marketed and sold repeatedly. This one-and-done approach reduces the stress and time associated with traditional revenue-generating methods, allowing for a more balanced lifestyle.

Automated lead generation strategies play a crucial role in establishing passive income through webinars. By utilizing tools that capture leads and nurture them via email marketing automation, businesses can build a database of prospects who are interested in their offerings. Once leads are engaged with relevant content and value-driven communications, they are more likely to convert during the webinar. This seamless integration of lead generation and nurturing ensures that the passive income stream remains consistent.

Content repurposing is another vital aspect of maximizing passive income through webinars. By transforming existing content into various formats—such as blog posts, social media snippets, and video clips—entrepreneurs can drive traffic to their webinar funnels. This multi-channel approach not only enhances visibility but also increases the chances of attracting a diverse audience. As more people view the webinars, the potential for passive income grows, reinforcing the importance of a strategic content marketing plan.

Ultimately, understanding the key components of passive income allows individuals to create effective automated webinar systems. This includes analyzing metrics to refine performance, crafting compelling webinar scripts, and integrating affiliate marketing strategies to boost earnings further. By mastering these elements, entrepreneurs can unlock the true potential of their passive income streams, ensuring that their automated webinars work tirelessly for them, even while they enjoy the freedom that comes with financial independence.

The Rise of Webinars in Online Marketing

The rise of webinars in online marketing has transformed the way businesses engage with their audiences, presenting an innovative means to deliver content, promote products, and generate leads. Initially used for educational purposes, webinars have evolved into a powerful marketing tool that allows brands to connect with potential customers in a more interactive and personal manner. With the advent of advanced technologies and platforms, hosting webinars has become more accessible, enabling marketers to reach wider audiences without the geographical limitations of traditional events.

One significant factor contributing to the popularity of webinars is their ability to provide value while simultaneously promoting a brand's offerings. By leveraging the "Lazy Webinar" method, marketers can create high-quality content that resonates with their target audience, all while automating the process for passive income generation. This approach not only saves time but also maximizes the potential for lead generation, as prospects can engage with the content on their own schedule. The ease of recording and repurposing webinars further enhances this method, allowing marketers to extend the reach of their message across multiple platforms.

In the realm of automated lead generation strategies, webinars serve as an effective mechanism for nurturing prospects through the sales funnel. By offering valuable insights and actionable advice during a webinar, businesses can build trust and credibility with potential customers. This trust is crucial when it comes to converting leads into paying customers. Additionally, the integration of email marketing automation with webinars ensures that interested participants are effectively followed up with, increasing the likelihood of conversions and fostering long-term relationships.

Furthermore, creating high-converting webinar funnels is essential for maximizing the effectiveness of this marketing strategy. A well-structured funnel guides potential customers from the initial awareness stage to the final purchase decision, simplifying the journey and enhancing user experience. Incorporating niche-specific topics can also significantly improve engagement, as tailored content speaks directly to the interests and pain points of the target audience. This specificity not only boosts attendance rates but also encourages participants to take action, whether that be signing up for a newsletter or making a purchase.

Finally, the success of webinars can be amplified through the strategic use of social media for traffic generation. Promoting webinars on platforms where the target audience spends their time increases visibility and participation. Crafting compelling webinar scripts that highlight key benefits and address common objections can further attract attendees. Analyzing webinar metrics post-event allows marketers to refine their strategies, ensuring continuous improvement. By integrating affiliate marketing with automated webinars, businesses can also tap into additional revenue streams, making webinars a multifaceted tool for building passive income.

Benefits of the Lazy Webinar Approach

The Lazy Webinar approach offers a streamlined method for generating passive income through automated presentations. Unlike traditional webinars that demand real-time attendance and engagement, this approach allows creators to record their content once and distribute it repeatedly. This one-and-done model not only saves time but also eliminates the stress associated with live presentations. By leveraging automation, entrepreneurs can focus on other aspects of their business while still attracting leads and making sales.

Another advantage of the Lazy Webinar method is its impact on lead generation strategies. By utilizing evergreen webinars, businesses can continuously draw in new prospects without the need for constant effort. These pre-recorded sessions can be promoted through various channels, including email marketing, social media, and website traffic. As a result, the Lazy Webinar method creates a consistent flow of leads, ultimately enhancing the potential for conversions and sales over time.

Email marketing automation plays a crucial role in maximizing the effectiveness of the Lazy Webinar approach. By nurturing leads through automated email sequences, businesses can engage with their audience before and after the webinar. This ensures that potential customers receive valuable information and reminders, increasing the likelihood of attendance and participation. Additionally, automated follow-ups can capitalize on the interest generated during the webinar, leading to higher conversion rates and sustained engagement.

Creating high-converting webinar funnels is another significant benefit of the Lazy Webinar method. A well-structured funnel guides potential customers from initial interest to final purchase seamlessly. By integrating persuasive call-to-actions, effective landing pages, and compelling content, entrepreneurs can optimize their sales process. The Lazy Webinar format allows for easy testing and tweaking of these funnels, ensuring that businesses can adapt their strategies based on real-time analytics and metrics.

Finally, the Lazy Webinar approach is an excellent opportunity for content repurposing and niche-specific marketing. Once a webinar is recorded, it can be transformed into various content formats, such as blog posts, social media snippets, or email campaigns. This not only maximizes the reach of the initial content but also keeps the audience engaged across different platforms. Furthermore, by selecting niche-specific topics, entrepreneurs can tailor their webinars to meet the needs and interests of their target market, increasing relevance and connection with potential customers.

Chapter 2: Setting Up Your Automated Webinar

Choosing the Right Webinar Platform

When selecting the right webinar platform for your passive income strategy, it's essential to consider several key factors that align with your goals and audience. First, assess the platform's features in relation to the specific needs of the "Lazy Webinar" method. Look for functionalities such as automated registration processes, customizable landing pages, and the ability to host pre-recorded webinars. These features will streamline your workflow and enhance the user experience for attendees, allowing you to focus on creating valuable content rather than managing logistics during the event.

User experience is another critical aspect to evaluate. A platform should be intuitive and easy to navigate, both for you as the host and for your audience. Complicated interfaces can deter potential attendees, leading to lower engagement rates. Opt for platforms that provide clear instructions and support, as well as a seamless registration process. Additionally, consider the ability to integrate with your existing tools, such as email marketing software, CRM systems, or payment processors, which can significantly improve your automated lead generation strategies.

Security and reliability are paramount when choosing a webinar platform, especially when handling sensitive attendee information. Look for platforms that offer robust security measures, including encryption and GDPR compliance. A reliable platform will ensure that your webinars run smoothly without unexpected technical issues, which can disrupt your automated processes and negatively impact your audience's experience. Research user reviews and consider conducting a trial run to test the platform's performance before committing.

Cost is also an important factor, as budget constraints can influence your choice. While free platforms may seem appealing, they often come with limitations that could hinder your automation goals. Assess the pricing plans of various platforms, focusing on the features that are most relevant to your needs. Investing in a quality platform that offers comprehensive features can pay off in the long run by enhancing your webinar's effectiveness and maximizing your passive income potential.

Finally, consider the level of customer support provided by the platform. As you navigate the complexities of automated webinars, having access to responsive customer service can be invaluable. Look for platforms that offer multiple support channels, such as live chat, email, or phone support, to resolve any issues quickly. A platform that prioritizes customer service will not only help you troubleshoot technical problems but also provide guidance on best practices for crafting compelling webinar scripts and analyzing metrics to improve performance.

Creating Your Webinar Content

Creating engaging and valuable content for your webinar is essential to ensure that it resonates with your audience and achieves its goals. Start by identifying the primary objective of your webinar. Are you aiming to educate your audience, sell a product, or generate leads? Once you have a clear goal in mind, tailor your content to meet the specific needs and interests of your target audience. Research their pain points, preferences, and questions to create content that addresses their challenges and provides actionable solutions.

When structuring your webinar content, consider the flow of information. Begin with a strong introduction that captures attention and sets the stage for what attendees can expect. Clearly outline the topics you will cover, and establish your credibility by sharing your expertise and personal anecdotes related to the subject. A well-organized presentation not only keeps your audience engaged but also enhances their understanding of the material, increasing the likelihood of conversion at the end of the session.

Visual aids play a crucial role in maintaining audience interest and reinforcing your message. Use slides, images, and videos to complement your spoken content and illustrate key points effectively. Ensure your visuals are high-quality and relevant to the topic. Avoid overcrowded slides; instead, focus on simplicity and clarity. Integrate bullet points, graphs, and charts to highlight important data, making it easier for your audience to digest the information.

Another important aspect of creating your webinar content is crafting a compelling narrative. Storytelling can significantly enhance engagement, allowing your audience to connect emotionally with the material. Weave relevant stories or case studies into your presentation to illustrate your points and demonstrate real-world applications of your strategies. This approach not only captivates your audience but also helps them visualize how they can implement what they learn in their own lives or businesses.

Lastly, always include a strong call to action at the end of your webinar. This is your opportunity to guide attendees on the next steps they should take, whether it's signing up for a newsletter, purchasing a product, or booking a consultation. Make it easy for them to follow through by providing clear instructions and links. By focusing on creating well-structured, engaging, and actionable content for your webinar, you set the foundation for a successful presentation that not only informs but also converts.

Recording Your Webinar

Recording your webinar is a crucial step in the Lazy Webinar method, as it allows you to create a high-quality, reusable asset that can generate passive income over time. To start, ensure you have the right tools and software in place. Popular webinar platforms like Zoom, WebinarJam, and EverWebinar offer built-in recording features, making it easy to capture your presentation along with any visual aids or screen sharing. Before you begin, familiarize yourself with the settings to optimize video and audio quality, as these factors significantly impact viewer experience. A clear, crisp recording will not only enhance engagement but also reflect professionalism, encouraging viewers to trust your content.

Preparation is key to a successful recording. Outline your presentation and rehearse it multiple times to ensure a smooth delivery. Pay attention to your pacing, tone, and body language. Effective webinars often rely on interactive elements, so plan how you will engage your audience during the session. Consider incorporating polls, Q&A segments, or chat interactions to maintain interest. Additionally, keep your environment distraction-free; ensure good lighting and minimize background noise. A well-prepared presentation not only improves the recording quality but also helps establish your authority in your niche.

During the recording, consider your audience's experience. Start with a strong introduction that outlines what participants can expect to learn. This sets the stage for your content and encourages viewers to stay engaged. Throughout the webinar, maintain a conversational tone and use storytelling techniques to make your points relatable. Remember to address potential pain points and provide actionable solutions. This not only enhances the value of your content but also increases the likelihood of converting viewers into leads or customers.

Once your webinar is recorded, the next step is editing. Editing helps you refine the content, removing any mistakes or long pauses that may detract from the overall flow. Utilize editing software to add visual elements such as slides, graphics, or call-to-action buttons that can enhance viewer engagement. You may also want to incorporate background music or sound effects to create a more dynamic viewing experience. Proper editing can transform a good webinar into a great one, making it more appealing for future viewers and maximizing your passive income potential.

Finally, after recording and editing your webinar, it's essential to implement a robust distribution strategy. Upload the final product to your webinar platform and create a dedicated landing page for it, optimizing the page for SEO to attract organic traffic. Leverage your email marketing list to promote the recorded webinar and encourage sign-ups. Additionally, consider using social media channels to share snippets or highlights of the webinar, driving traffic back to your landing page. By effectively recording, editing, and promoting your webinar, you can create a powerful tool for automated lead generation and passive income, aligning perfectly with the Lazy Webinar method.

Chapter 3: Automated Lead Generation Strategies

Building Your Target Audience

Building your target audience is a crucial first step in leveraging the Lazy Webinar Method for passive income. Understanding who your ideal audience is allows you to tailor your content and marketing strategies effectively. Begin by identifying the demographics and psychographics of your potential viewers. Consider their age, gender, location, interests, and pain points. This information helps you create a persona that encapsulates your target audience, guiding your content and promotional efforts.

Once you have a clear understanding of your ideal audience, it's essential to engage them through various channels. Automated lead generation strategies can assist in attracting the right viewers to your webinars. Use tools such as landing pages, social media ads, and email campaigns to capture leads. By offering valuable content, like free guides or checklists, you can entice your audience to sign up for your webinars. Remember that the goal is to build a list of engaged subscribers who are interested in your niche, setting the stage for successful automated marketing.

Email marketing automation plays a significant role in nurturing your audience after they've signed up. Develop a series of automated welcome emails that introduce your brand and convey the benefits of attending your webinars. This series should also provide additional value, such as links to relevant blog posts or resources. Regularly segment your email list based on engagement levels and interests to personalize your communications further. This approach not only keeps your audience engaged but also increases the likelihood of converting them into loyal customers.

Creating high-converting webinar funnels requires a deep understanding of your audience's needs and preferences. Use the insights gained from audience analysis to craft compelling webinar topics that resonate with them. Focus on addressing their challenges and providing actionable solutions. Additionally, consider repurposing content from previous webinars and adapting it to cater to different segments of your audience. This strategy not only saves time but also ensures that you are consistently delivering valuable content that aligns with your audience's interests.

Finally, leveraging social media for webinar traffic is essential for expanding your reach. Identify the platforms where your target audience is most active, and create shareable content that promotes your webinars. Use engaging visuals and compelling calls to action to encourage sharing among their networks. Analyzing webinar metrics will also inform your audience-building efforts, allowing you to refine your approach based on what resonates most with viewers. By continuously evaluating and adapting your strategies, you can effectively build and maintain a targeted audience that drives passive income through the Lazy Webinar Method.

Opt-in Pages and Lead Magnets

Opt-in pages serve as a critical entry point for potential leads in the context of the Lazy Webinar Method. These pages are designed to capture visitor information, typically through a simple form that requests an email address in exchange for valuable content or offers. The effectiveness of an opt-in page relies heavily on its design, messaging, and the perceived value of the lead magnet offered. A compelling headline, clear and concise copy, and an attractive layout can significantly increase conversion rates, encouraging visitors to submit their information and join your email list.

Lead magnets are pivotal to the success of your opt-in pages. A lead magnet is any resource or content that provides value to your audience in exchange for their contact details. This could be an eBook, a checklist, a video series, or exclusive access to a webinar. The key is to ensure that the lead magnet addresses a specific pain point or need within your target niche. For example, if your audience is seeking automated lead generation strategies, offering a straightforward guide on how to set up an automated system can entice them to opt-in. The more relevant and useful the lead magnet, the higher the likelihood of converting visitors into leads.

Once you have established your opt-in page and lead magnet, integrating them into your overall webinar funnel is essential. The opt-in page should seamlessly direct users to the webinar registration page, creating a fluid experience that maximizes engagement. This transition is crucial in maintaining interest and ensuring that potential leads are aware of the upcoming webinar. Additionally, follow-up emails should be scheduled to nurture these leads further, providing them with additional resources and reminders about the webinar, ultimately increasing attendance rates.

To enhance the performance of your opt-in pages, testing and optimization are vital. Experimenting with different headlines, images, and calls to action can reveal what resonates best with your audience. A/B testing is an effective strategy to identify which variations of your opt-in page yield the highest conversion rates. Furthermore, analyzing metrics from your opt-in forms can provide insights into user behavior, allowing you to refine your approach continually. This data-driven strategy will lead to a more effective lead generation process and, consequently, a more successful passive income stream through your webinars.

Lastly, leveraging social media to promote your opt-in pages can significantly boost traffic and lead generation. Creating shareable content that links to your opt-in page can help attract a broader audience. Platforms like Facebook, Instagram, and LinkedIn offer targeted advertising options that can be utilized to reach specific demographics interested in your niche. Engaging with your audience through social media can also build rapport and trust, making them more likely to opt-in for your lead magnet. By creating a robust ecosystem of opt-in pages, lead magnets, and social media strategies, you will enhance your ability to generate leads and maximize the potential of your lazy webinars.

Driving Traffic to Your Webinar

Driving traffic to your webinar is a crucial step in ensuring its success and maximizing your passive income potential. To effectively attract the right audience, it is essential to utilize a combination of strategies tailored to your niche. Begin by identifying your target demographic and understanding where they spend their time online. This knowledge will help you focus your promotional efforts on platforms and channels that resonate with your audience, increasing the likelihood of attendance and engagement during your webinar.

One effective method for driving traffic is through automated lead generation strategies. By creating valuable content such as ebooks, guides, or checklists related to your webinar topic, you can entice potential attendees to sign up for your mailing list. Once you have their contact information, you can nurture these leads through a series of automated email sequences designed to build interest and anticipation for your webinar. Utilize email marketing automation tools to segment your audience based on their interests, allowing for personalized messaging that speaks directly to their needs.

Another powerful avenue for traffic generation is leveraging social media platforms. Each platform offers unique opportunities to promote your webinar and reach a wider audience. Create engaging posts that highlight the benefits of attending your webinar, and consider using paid advertising to target specific demographics. Regularly share testimonials, sneak peeks of your content, and countdown reminders to keep your audience engaged. Additionally, consider collaborating with influencers in your niche to tap into their followers, thereby expanding your reach and driving more traffic to your registration page.

Content repurposing can also play a significant role in promoting your webinar. Transform existing content such as blog posts, podcasts, or videos into promotional materials that direct traffic to your webinar. For instance, if you have a popular blog post, create a corresponding video that discusses the same topic and includes a call-to-action inviting viewers to register for your webinar. This strategy not only helps you reach different segments of your audience but also reinforces your authority in your niche, making attendees more likely to register.

Finally, tracking and analyzing webinar metrics is vital for improving future traffic generation efforts. Use analytics tools to assess which traffic sources are most effective in driving registrations and attendance. Pay attention to metrics such as click-through rates, engagement levels, and conversion rates to refine your promotional strategies over time. By continuously testing different approaches and optimizing based on data, you can create a sustainable traffic-driving system that consistently attracts attendees to your automated webinars, ensuring a steady stream of passive income.

Chapter 4: Email Marketing Automation for Webinars

Crafting Your Email Sequence

Crafting your email sequence is a crucial component of the Lazy Webinar method, as it serves to build relationships with your audience and guide them toward taking action. The foundation of a successful email sequence lies in understanding your target audience and what motivates them. Start by segmenting your email list based on interests, demographics, or behavior. This allows you to tailor your messages and create personalized experiences that resonate with your subscribers. By knowing what challenges they face and what solutions you offer, you can craft emails that speak directly to their needs and desires.

Your email sequence should be designed to nurture leads and gradually lead them to your webinar. Begin with a welcome email that introduces yourself and sets expectations for what subscribers will receive. Follow this with a series of value-driven emails that provide insights, tips, or resources related to the topic of your webinar. This not only establishes your authority but also builds trust with your audience. Incorporating storytelling elements can make these emails more engaging and relatable, fostering a stronger connection with your readers.

As you progress through your email sequence, it's essential to create anticipation around your upcoming webinar. Utilize countdown timers, sneak peeks, or exclusive content to stimulate interest. Highlight the benefits of attending the webinar and what attendees will gain from it. Incorporate strong calls to action that direct readers to register, ensuring that the link stands out visually. Timing is also key; send reminders as the webinar approaches to keep it top-of-mind, while also providing additional value through supplementary emails that align with the content of the webinar.

Incorporating automated email marketing tools can streamline the process of crafting and sending your email sequence. Look for platforms that offer features such as segmentation, A/B testing, and analytics. These tools can help you optimize your emails for better performance and allow you to focus on creating quality content rather than manual tasks. Automated follow-ups can also be set up for attendees who missed the live session, ensuring that everyone has access to the materials and encourages future engagement.

Finally, analyze the performance of your email sequence to continually improve your strategy. Monitor open rates, click-through rates, and conversion rates to identify what resonates with your audience. Use these insights to refine your emails, testing different subject lines, content formats, or calls to action. By regularly assessing your email sequence's effectiveness, you can adapt and enhance your approach, ultimately leading to higher attendance at your webinars and increased passive income through your automated systems.

Triggering Automated Follow-ups

Triggering automated follow-ups is a crucial strategy within the "Lazy Webinar" method that enhances engagement and conversion rates. Once a potential attendee registers for your webinar, this is just the beginning of the interaction. Automated follow-ups allow you to nurture these leads without the need for constant manual effort. By utilizing email marketing automation, you can create a series of messages tailored to guide registrants through their journey, ultimately leading them towards taking the desired action, whether that's attending the webinar, purchasing a product, or signing up for a service.

The first step in crafting effective automated follow-ups is to segment your audience based on their behaviors and preferences. This segmentation allows you to send targeted messages that resonate more deeply with each group. For instance, those who registered but did not attend the webinar may require a different approach than those who attended but did not take further action. By personalizing your follow-up emails, you not only increase the likelihood of engagement but also demonstrate to your audience that you understand their specific needs and interests.

Incorporating a variety of content types into your automated follow-ups can significantly boost engagement rates. Consider including helpful resources, such as downloadable guides, video snippets from the webinar, or links to relevant blog posts. This content repurposing not only provides added value to your audience but also reinforces the information shared in the webinar. Additionally, you can integrate social proof by sharing testimonials or case studies that highlight the success others have experienced by implementing the strategies discussed in your webinar.

Timing is another critical factor when it comes to automated follow-ups. The effectiveness of your messages can be greatly influenced by when they are sent. A common strategy is to send an immediate follow-up after the webinar, thanking attendees for their participation and offering additional resources. Subsequent follow-ups can be scheduled over the following days or weeks, gradually increasing urgency for any offers or calls to action. This pacing helps to keep your webinar top of mind and encourages recipients to take action before the opportunity closes.

Finally, analyzing the performance of your automated follow-ups is essential for ongoing optimization. By reviewing metrics such as open rates, click-through rates, and conversion rates, you can gain insights into what resonates with your audience and what doesn't. This data-driven approach enables you to refine your follow-up strategy continuously, ensuring that your automated messages remain effective and relevant. By applying these insights, you can enhance the overall performance of your "Lazy Webinar" system, driving more passive income through well-timed and strategically crafted follow-ups.

Segmenting Your Audience for Better Results

Segmenting your audience is a critical step in maximizing the effectiveness of your automated webinars. By understanding the distinct characteristics, interests, and needs of different audience segments, you can tailor your messaging and content to resonate more deeply with each group. This approach not only enhances engagement but also increases the likelihood of conversion, making your passive income efforts more successful. Each segment should be identified based on relevant criteria, such as demographics, past behavior, and specific interests related to your niche.

One effective method of audience segmentation is to analyze the data collected from previous interactions. For instance, if a segment of your audience has shown interest in automated lead generation strategies, you can create targeted content that speaks directly to their pain points and aspirations. This could include offering solutions to common challenges they face or showcasing success stories from others in similar situations. By providing information that is relevant and useful, you build trust and authority, which can significantly impact their decision-making process.

Email marketing automation plays a pivotal role in reaching segmented audiences. By setting up tailored email sequences for each segment, you can deliver personalized content that aligns with their specific interests and needs. For example, a segment focused on affiliate marketing may benefit from insights on integrating affiliate offers into webinars, while another segment interested in high-converting webinar funnels might require detailed strategies on optimizing their conversion rates. This level of personalization fosters a connection with your audience and demonstrates that you understand their unique challenges.

In addition to email marketing, leveraging social media can enhance your segmentation strategy. By analyzing engagement metrics across different platforms, you can identify which segments are most active and receptive to your content. This information allows you to tailor your social media campaigns to target these specific groups, ensuring that your promotional efforts are aligned with their preferences. Additionally, using social media analytics can help you refine your audience segments over time, ensuring that your strategies remain effective as market dynamics change.

Finally, continuous analysis of webinar metrics is essential for improving your segmentation efforts. Metrics such as attendance rates, engagement levels, and conversion rates can provide valuable insights into how well your content resonates with each audience segment. By regularly reviewing this data, you can make informed adjustments to your segmentation strategy, enhancing the overall effectiveness of your automated webinars. This ongoing refinement process not only boosts your passive income potential but also positions you as a responsive and customer-centric provider in your niche.

Chapter 5: Creating High-Converting Webinar Funnels

Mapping Out Your Funnel

Mapping out your funnel is a critical step in effectively implementing the "Lazy Webinar" method for generating passive income. A well-structured funnel guides potential customers through a seamless journey from initial awareness to final conversion. Start by identifying your target audience and their pain points. Understanding their needs will enable you to tailor your webinar content and marketing strategies to resonate with them, ultimately increasing engagement and conversion rates.

The next step involves outlining the stages of your funnel: awareness, interest, decision, and action. At the awareness stage, leverage social media, blog posts, and other channels to drive traffic to your webinar landing page. Use compelling headlines and visuals to capture attention. The interest stage is where you offer valuable content that addresses your audience's challenges, encouraging them to register for your webinar. This can include lead magnets such as eBooks or free courses that entice potential participants to share their contact information.

Once attendees register for your webinar, the decision stage comes into play. This is where email marketing automation becomes essential. Send a series of pre-webinar emails that build anticipation and provide valuable insights related to your webinar topic. These emails can include reminders, testimonials, and sneak peeks of what attendees can expect, which help to reaffirm their decision to attend. Additionally, consider using retargeting ads on social media to remind those who showed interest but did not register.

After the webinar concludes, the action stage aims to convert attendees into paying customers. Craft a compelling follow-up email sequence that highlights key takeaways from the webinar and presents a clear call to action. This could be an exclusive offer or a limited-time discount on related products or services. Incorporate testimonials and case studies to build trust and credibility, making it easier for attendees to take that final step towards purchasing.

Finally, continuously analyze your funnel's performance to identify areas for improvement. Utilize metrics such as registration rates, attendance rates, and post-webinar conversion rates to gauge the effectiveness of your strategies. Tools and software for webinar automation can help streamline this process, enabling you to track engagement and gather valuable insights. By refining your funnel based on data-driven decisions, you can optimize your lazy webinar method for greater efficiency and increased passive income.

Optimizing Landing Pages

Optimizing landing pages is crucial for the success of any automated webinar strategy. A landing page serves as the first point of interaction for potential attendees, and its design and content can significantly influence conversion rates. To optimize these pages effectively, it is essential to focus on key elements such as clarity, relevance, and persuasive messaging. A clear headline that communicates the value of the webinar is paramount. It should immediately convey what the attendee will gain by signing up, compelling them to take action.

In addition to a strong headline, the use of engaging visuals and a clean layout can enhance user experience. Visual elements, such as images or videos, should complement the overall message without overwhelming the visitor. A visually appealing landing page that guides the visitor's eye towards the call-to-action is more likely to convert. It's also important to ensure that the landing page is mobile-friendly, as many users will access it from their smartphones or tablets. A responsive design that adapts to different screen sizes can significantly reduce bounce rates.

The copy on the landing page must resonate with the target audience. Understanding the pain points and desires of your niche allows you to craft messages that speak directly to their needs. Incorporating testimonials or social proof can further enhance credibility and persuade potential attendees. Highlighting limited-time offers or exclusive bonuses can create urgency, motivating users to register immediately. The language should be clear and concise, avoiding jargon that may confuse or alienate visitors.

Incorporating effective SEO practices is another vital aspect of landing page optimization. This includes using relevant keywords and phrases that your target audience is searching for. Optimizing meta tags, alt text for images, and ensuring fast loading times can improve search engine rankings and drive more organic traffic to your landing page. Additionally, integrating analytics tools can help track user behavior on the page, providing insights into which elements are performing well and where improvements are needed.

Finally, continuous testing and iteration is essential for maintaining an optimized landing page. A/B testing different headlines, calls-to-action, and layouts can reveal what resonates best with your audience. Based on performance metrics, adjustments can be made to improve engagement and conversion rates over time. By understanding that optimization is an ongoing process, marketers can ensure their landing pages remain effective and aligned with evolving audience expectations, ultimately maximizing the potential for passive income through automated webinars.

Effective Call-to-Actions

Effective call-to-actions (CTAs) are crucial for guiding your audience toward the desired outcome in your automated webinars. They serve as the bridge between passive content consumption and active engagement, helping to convert viewers into leads or customers. A well-crafted CTA can significantly enhance the effectiveness of your webinar by providing clear directions on what the viewer should do next. The key is to ensure that your CTAs align with the overall goals of your webinar and resonate with the specific needs and desires of your target audience.

To create compelling CTAs, it is essential to understand your audience's motivations and pain points. Effective CTAs should address these directly, offering solutions that your webinar promises to deliver. Use language that is straightforward and action-oriented. Phrases like "Join now," "Download your free guide," or "Schedule your consultation today" create urgency and encourage immediate response. By embedding these CTAs at strategic points throughout your webinar, you can capture interest when viewers are most engaged, maximizing the likelihood of conversion.

Incorporating CTAs at different stages of your webinar is a powerful strategy. Early in the presentation, you might introduce a soft CTA that invites viewers to think about the benefits they will receive. As you progress, you can escalate to more direct CTAs that prompt immediate action, such as signing up for an email list or purchasing a product. Furthermore, a strong closing CTA can reinforce the value of your offering and remind viewers of the benefits they stand to gain by taking action now. This layered approach ensures that your audience remains engaged and receptive throughout the duration of the webinar.

Visual elements also play a significant role in the effectiveness of CTAs. Using contrasting colors, bold fonts, or eye-catching graphics can help your CTAs stand out on the screen. Additionally, consider placing CTAs in multiple formats, such as buttons, banners, or verbal prompts. This variety caters to different viewer preferences and reinforces the message through repetition. A well-designed CTA not only captures attention but also guides viewers seamlessly toward the next step in their journey.

Finally, measuring the effectiveness of your CTAs is essential for continuous improvement. Utilize webinar analytics tools to track click-through rates, conversion rates, and audience engagement metrics. This data will provide insights into which CTAs resonate most with your audience and allow you to refine your approach over time. By adopting a data-driven mindset, you can optimize your CTAs to enhance their impact, ultimately leading to greater automation success and increased passive income through your webinars.

Chapter 6: Content Repurposing for Webinar Promotion

Transforming Webinar Content into Blog Posts

Transforming webinar content into blog posts is a strategic approach that allows you to extend the life and reach of your original material. Webinars often contain valuable insights, expert knowledge, and engaging discussions that can be repurposed for a broader audience. By converting this content into blog posts, you not only enhance your content marketing strategy but also improve your search engine optimization (SEO) efforts. This process can lead to increased organic traffic and more opportunities for conversions.

To begin the transformation, review your webinar recording and identify key themes, insights, and actionable takeaways. Create an outline that highlights these points clearly, ensuring each section of the blog post corresponds to a segment of the webinar. This will help maintain the flow and coherence of the original content while allowing for additional expansion or clarification. Consider incorporating quotes or paraphrased statements from the webinar, as these can lend authority and credibility to your blog post.

Next, focus on optimizing your blog post for SEO. This involves conducting keyword research related to your webinar topic and strategically integrating these keywords throughout your content. Ensure that your headings, subheadings, and meta descriptions are also optimized for search engines. This not only helps your blog post rank better but also makes it easier for potential readers to find your content when searching for information related to your webinar's subject matter.

Incorporating visuals can significantly enhance the engagement of your blog post. Utilize screenshots from the webinar, infographics summarizing data or insights, and relevant images that complement your text. Visual elements can break up large blocks of text, making the post more reader-friendly. Additionally, embedding the webinar video or linking to it can provide readers with an option to consume the content in a different format, catering to varied preferences.

Finally, promote your newly created blog post across various channels to maximize its reach. Share it through your email marketing campaigns, social media platforms, and within your webinar follow-up sequences. Encourage your audience to engage with the post through comments or shares, fostering a community around your content. By effectively transforming webinar content into blog posts, you not only create additional assets for your marketing strategy but also establish yourself as a thought leader in your niche, paving the way for further passive income opportunities.

Creating Social Media Snippets

Creating social media snippets is an essential strategy for maximizing the reach and effectiveness of your lazy webinar. These snippets serve as bite-sized pieces of content that capture the essence of your webinar, enticing your audience to engage further. When crafting these snippets, it's vital to focus on the key takeaways or highlights from your webinar, ensuring they resonate with your target audience. This approach not only keeps your branding consistent but also provides a clear message that can drive traffic to your webinar funnel.

To begin, identify the main topics or pain points addressed in your webinar. These themes should align with your audience's interests and needs. For instance, if your webinar focuses on automated lead generation strategies, snippets could include statistics or quotes that underscore the effectiveness of these methods. Incorporating visual elements, such as engaging graphics or short video clips, can also enhance the appeal of these snippets, making them more likely to be shared across social media platforms.

Choosing the right social media channels is crucial for distributing your snippets effectively. Different platforms cater to different demographics and content styles. For example, Instagram and TikTok thrive on visually appealing content, while LinkedIn is more suited for professional insights and detailed discussions. Tailoring your snippets to fit the format and audience of each platform can significantly increase engagement and drive traffic back to your webinar registration page.

Timing and frequency of posting your snippets are also important considerations. An effective strategy involves sharing snippets at various intervals leading up to your webinar. This approach builds anticipation and keeps your content fresh in the minds of your audience. Additionally, consider using social media scheduling tools to automate the posting process. This allows you to maintain a consistent online presence without the need for constant manual updates.

Finally, monitor the performance of your social media snippets through analytics tools available on each platform. Understanding which snippets garner the most engagement can inform your future content creation strategies. By analyzing metrics such as likes, shares, comments, and click-through rates, you can refine your approach, ensuring your social media efforts continually align with your goals of driving traffic and generating passive income through the lazy webinar method.

Utilizing Video Clips for Promotion

Utilizing video clips for promotion can significantly enhance the effectiveness of your marketing strategy, particularly within the framework of the Lazy Webinar Method. Video content has become an essential tool for capturing attention and conveying information quickly. By integrating short, engaging video clips into your promotional efforts, you can effectively communicate the value of your webinars while also showcasing your expertise in the niche. These clips can serve as teasers or highlights from your webinars, enticing potential attendees to sign up and participate.

When creating video clips for promotional purposes, it is crucial to keep your target audience in mind. Tailor your content to address their specific pain points, desires, and interests related to passive income and automated strategies. For instance, a brief video that outlines the benefits of using automated lead generation strategies can quickly resonate with viewers, encouraging them to explore your offerings further. Additionally, utilizing testimonials or success stories from past webinar participants can enhance credibility and build trust, making your promotions more compelling.

Social media platforms are ideal channels for distributing your promotional video clips. By sharing these videos on platforms such as Facebook, Instagram, and LinkedIn, you can reach a wider audience and engage with potential attendees where they are most active. Incorporating relevant hashtags and strategically posting during peak engagement times can further increase visibility. Moreover, consider utilizing paid advertising options on these platforms to amplify your reach and target specific demographics that align with your niche.

Email marketing is another powerful avenue for promoting your webinars through video clips. Including a short video in your email campaigns can significantly improve open and click-through rates. Ensure that the video is concise and includes a clear call to action, directing viewers to register for the webinar. This combination of engaging video content and direct promotion can lead to higher conversion rates and increased attendance, maximizing the passive income potential of your webinars.

Finally, analyze the performance of your promotional video clips to continually refine your strategy. Utilize metrics such as viewer retention rates, engagement levels, and conversion statistics to assess which types of content resonate most with your audience. By understanding what works, you can optimize future video promotions, ensuring they effectively drive traffic to your webinars and contribute to a sustainable passive income stream. Embracing video clips in your promotional efforts not only enhances engagement but also establishes a stronger connection with your audience, ultimately leading to greater success in your automated webinar initiatives.

Chapter 7: Niche-Specific Webinar Topics for Passive Income

Identifying Profitable Niches

Identifying a profitable niche is crucial for anyone looking to implement the Lazy Webinar Method effectively. A niche represents a specific segment of the market where your products or services can stand out and attract a targeted audience. By honing in on a niche, you can tailor your content, marketing strategies, and webinars to meet the unique needs and interests of that audience. This focused approach not only enhances engagement but also increases the likelihood of converting leads into customers.

To start identifying a profitable niche, consider your areas of expertise and interests. Reflect on what you are passionate about, as enthusiasm can translate into more authentic and persuasive presentations. Additionally, analyze market trends and demands. Research tools such as Google Trends, social media conversations, and keyword analysis to discover which topics are gaining traction. By aligning your interests with market demand, you can create content that resonates well and stands out among the competition.

Another effective strategy is to explore existing gaps in the market. Look for underserved audiences or topics within your broader field. For instance, while many may be covering general webinar automation strategies, there may be fewer resources addressing niche-specific webinar topics tailored for unique industries. By filling these gaps, you can position yourself as an authority in that niche, leading to more opportunities for passive income through automated webinars.

It's also essential to evaluate the profitability of your chosen niche. This involves researching potential competitors and their offerings. Analyzing their success can provide insight into what works and what doesn't. Additionally, consider the monetization possibilities within your niche. Can you integrate affiliate marketing, offer premium content, or promote related products? A niche with multiple revenue streams will provide greater opportunities for sustainable income.

Finally, test and refine your niche selection through pilot webinars or content pieces. Gather feedback and analyze metrics to determine engagement levels and potential profitability. This iterative process allows you to adapt and fine-tune your approach based on real-world data. Ultimately, identifying a profitable niche is not just about finding a topic; it's about creating a focused strategy that aligns with your goals while effectively meeting the needs of your target audience.

Researching Audience Pain Points

Understanding your audience's pain points is crucial when developing a successful passive income strategy through the Lazy Webinar method. Pain points represent the specific challenges or problems that your target audience faces. Identifying these issues enables you to tailor your content, including webinars, to address their needs directly. By focusing on these pain points, you can effectively position your automated webinars as solutions, increasing engagement and conversion rates.

To research audience pain points, start by gathering data from various sources. Online forums and social media groups related to your niche can provide valuable insights into what your audience is struggling with. Pay attention to the questions being asked, the complaints being voiced, and the solutions sought. Additionally, consider conducting surveys or interviews with your existing audience or potential customers. This direct feedback can yield rich information about their challenges and desires, allowing you to create content that resonates.

Another effective method is to analyze your competitors. Review their webinars, marketing materials, and customer testimonials to identify common themes in the pain points they address. This not only helps you understand what is currently being discussed within your niche, but it also allows you to find gaps in the market where you can position your offerings. A thorough competitive analysis will highlight both the pain points that are saturated and those that are underrepresented, guiding you toward unique angles for your content.

Once you have gathered sufficient data, categorize the pain points into specific themes or topics. This categorization can help streamline your content creation process, making it easier to develop targeted webinar topics that align with your audience's needs. For instance, if you discover that many potential attendees struggle with automated lead generation strategies, consider crafting a webinar that addresses this issue directly. By providing actionable solutions, you can enhance your audience's experience and improve the likelihood of conversion.

Finally, continuously monitor and revisit your audience's pain points. The online landscape is ever-changing, and so are the challenges faced by your audience. Regularly updating your research will ensure that your webinars remain relevant and valuable. Incorporating feedback from past webinars will also help you refine your understanding of audience needs. By staying attuned to these dynamics, you can maintain a strong connection with your audience, ultimately leading to sustained passive income through your Lazy Webinar strategy.

Validating Your Webinar Topic

Validating your webinar topic is a critical step in ensuring that your effort in creating and automating a webinar translates into passive income. The first step in this validation process is to conduct market research. Understand your target audience's pain points, interests, and desires. Utilize surveys, polls, and social media conversations to gather insights. This data will help you identify what topics resonate with your audience, ensuring that your webinar addresses a real need. By aligning your content with audience expectations, you increase the likelihood of engagement and conversion.

Next, consider analyzing existing webinars within your niche. Look for successful webinars that have a high level of engagement and conversions. Take note of the topics they cover and the presentation styles they adopt. By examining what works for others, you can adapt and innovate your approach. Pay attention to viewer feedback and comments, as they can provide valuable clues about what aspects of the topic are most appealing or problematic. This competitive analysis will not only validate your chosen topic but also inspire unique angles to present it.

After gathering preliminary data, it's crucial to test your topic with a smaller audience before launching the full webinar. This can be done through mini-webinars or live Q&A sessions where you discuss your topic in a condensed format. The feedback you receive during these sessions can be instrumental in refining your content. Pay attention to audience engagement, questions asked, and reactions. This process will help you gauge interest levels and adjust your approach accordingly, ensuring that when you launch your automated webinar, it is fine-tuned to meet audience expectations.

Another effective method of validation is to leverage your email list or social media following. Create a few compelling subject lines or key points about your proposed topic and use them in a survey or social media poll. This direct engagement with your audience allows you to assess interest levels and gather preferences. Additionally, it builds anticipation for your upcoming webinar, as your audience feels involved in the topic selection process. Such engagement not only validates your topic but also fosters a sense of community and investment among your followers.

Finally, once you have validated your topic, ensure that it aligns with your overall business goals and passive income strategies. The topic should not only attract immediate interest but also have the potential for future monetization through automated lead generation and affiliate marketing. Consider how the content can be repurposed across different platforms and formats to maximize its reach and effectiveness. By ensuring that your webinar topic fits seamlessly into your broader marketing and income strategies, you set the stage for sustainable passive income generation.

Chapter 8: Tools and Software for Webinar Automation

Essential Webinar Software

When selecting essential webinar software, it is crucial to understand the specific features that will support the Lazy Webinar method effectively. The software you choose must facilitate seamless automation, ensuring that your webinars run without requiring your active participation after the initial setup. Key features to look for include automated registration and reminder emails, user-friendly interfaces for both hosts and attendees, and reliable video streaming capabilities. Additionally, integration with email marketing platforms is essential for nurturing leads generated through your webinars and maintaining engagement with your audience.

Another important aspect is the ability to create high-converting webinar funnels. The software should provide tools for designing landing pages that not only attract visitors but also convert them into registrants. A/B testing capabilities can help refine these funnels, allowing you to identify which elements resonate most with your audience. Furthermore, tracking registration sources can provide insights into which marketing channels are most effective, enabling you to allocate resources more efficiently.

Content repurposing is another vital strategy in maximizing the value of your webinars. Look for software that allows you to record sessions easily and edit them for reuse across different platforms. This feature can help you create promotional clips, highlight reels, or even full-on courses from your webinar content. The ability to share recorded webinars on social media or embed them in your website further amplifies your reach and can drive additional traffic to your automated funnels.

Analyzing webinar metrics is essential for improving performance over time. The right software should offer comprehensive analytics that track key performance indicators such as attendance rates, engagement levels, and conversion rates. Understanding these metrics will enable you to make informed decisions about future webinars, including topic selection, presentation style, and promotional strategies. Regularly reviewing this data will help you refine your approach and increase your passive income potential.

Lastly, integrating affiliate marketing with your automated webinars can significantly enhance your income streams. Choose software that allows easy integration of affiliate links and tracking tools. This will enable you to promote relevant products or services during your webinars, creating additional revenue opportunities. By leveraging the power of affiliate marketing alongside your passive webinar strategy, you can create a more robust and sustainable income model that aligns perfectly with the Lazy Webinar method.

Automation Tools for Marketing

Automation tools for marketing have drastically transformed the way businesses operate, particularly when it comes to webinars. They enable marketers to streamline processes, engage audiences, and generate passive income with minimal effort. For individuals utilizing the Lazy Webinar Method, selecting the right automation tools can significantly enhance their marketing strategies. These tools allow for the seamless creation, promotion, and execution of webinars, ensuring that marketers can focus on content quality rather than administrative tasks.

One crucial area where automation tools excel is in lead generation. Automated lead generation strategies help capture potential attendees' information without requiring constant manual input. Tools like landing page builders and lead magnets can be integrated into a user's website or social media platforms, enabling them to gather leads efficiently. Once captured, these leads can be nurtured through automated email sequences that provide value and encourage registration for upcoming webinars. This not only saves time but also ensures that leads are consistently engaged throughout the marketing funnel.

Email marketing automation is another vital component of successful webinar promotion. By utilizing automation tools, marketers can create targeted email campaigns that nurture leads and drive traffic to their webinars. These tools allow for personalized messaging based on user behavior, ensuring that recipients receive relevant content that resonates with their interests. Automated reminders, follow-ups, and feedback requests can be scheduled in advance, ensuring that attendees remain engaged and informed throughout the entire webinar experience, thus increasing the chances of conversion.

Creating high-converting webinar funnels also benefits greatly from marketing automation tools. These platforms often come equipped with analytics features that help marketers track user behavior and optimize their funnels for better performance. By analyzing metrics such as registration rates, attendance rates, and post-webinar engagement, marketers can identify areas for improvement and make data-driven decisions. This continuous cycle of analysis and optimization leads to improved funnel effectiveness and higher passive income potential.

Finally, leveraging social media for traffic generation becomes more manageable with automation tools. Scheduling posts, creating engaging content, and monitoring social media interactions can all be automated, allowing marketers to maintain a consistent online presence without the need for daily involvement. Tools that integrate social media management with webinar registration can streamline the process further, enabling marketers to create cohesive campaigns that drive traffic to their webinars effectively. By harnessing these automation tools, individuals can maximize their efforts, ensuring that their passive income strategies through webinars are both effective and efficient.

Integrating Technology for Seamless Performance

Integrating technology effectively is crucial for achieving seamless performance in the context of the Lazy Webinar method. By leveraging various tools and platforms, you can automate numerous aspects of your webinar process, ensuring that your audience experiences a smooth and engaging presentation without requiring constant manual input. The right technology not only saves you time but also enhances the overall quality of your webinars, allowing you to focus on content creation and strategic planning.

One of the primary components of successful webinar automation is the use of reliable software for hosting and broadcasting your sessions. Choosing a platform that offers user-friendly interfaces, robust analytics, and seamless integration with other marketing tools can significantly improve your workflow. For instance, platforms like Zoom, WebinarJam, or EverWebinar provide features that allow for easy recording, editing, and replaying of webinars, which is essential for creating a one-and-done automated system. These platforms also facilitate real-time audience interaction through Q&A sessions and polls, enhancing engagement while minimizing the need for live intervention.

Automated lead generation strategies are another area where technology plays a vital role. Utilizing advanced tools for capturing and nurturing leads can streamline the process of attracting potential participants to your webinars. Email marketing automation platforms such as Mailchimp or ConvertKit can help you design targeted campaigns that not only promote your upcoming webinars but also follow up with attendees afterward. By automating your email sequences, you can ensure that your audience receives timely reminders, resources, and offers, ultimately increasing conversion rates without additional effort on your part.

Social media integration is also essential for driving traffic to your webinars. Tools like Hootsuite or Buffer allow you to schedule and manage your social media posts efficiently, ensuring consistent promotion across platforms. The ability to analyze the performance of your social media campaigns through built-in analytics means you can adjust your strategies based on real-time data, focusing your efforts on the channels that yield the best results. By strategically leveraging social media, you can expand your reach and attract a larger audience to your automated webinars.

Finally, integrating affiliate marketing into your automated webinar strategy can amplify your passive income potential. Utilizing affiliate software, such as Tapfiliate or Refersion, allows you to manage partnerships seamlessly, tracking conversions and commissions without manual oversight. By promoting relevant affiliate products during your webinars, you can create additional revenue streams while providing value to your audience. This integration not only enhances your earnings but also improves the overall experience for attendees, as they are introduced to curated products that complement the content of your webinars.

Chapter 9: Leveraging Social Media for Webinar Traffic

Utilizing Facebook and Instagram

Utilizing Facebook and Instagram effectively can significantly enhance your passive income strategy through the Lazy Webinar method. These platforms offer vast audiences and powerful advertising tools, making them ideal for driving traffic to your automated webinars. Begin by establishing a strong presence on both platforms, focusing on creating engaging content that resonates with your target audience. Utilize Facebook groups and pages to build a community around your niche, while Instagram's visual nature allows you to showcase your content in a captivating way. Regularly posting valuable information, behind-the-scenes looks, and testimonials can help build trust and interest in your webinars.

When it comes to Facebook, leveraging its advertising capabilities is essential for reaching a broader audience. Use Facebook Ads to target specific demographics that align with your ideal customer profile. Experiment with different ad formats, such as video ads or carousel ads, to see which resonates most with your audience. Additionally, retargeting campaigns can remind those who have shown interest in your webinars but have not yet signed up. Creating compelling ad copy and visuals that highlight the benefits of attending your webinar is crucial for generating leads and converting interest into registrations.

Instagram, on the other hand, thrives on visually appealing content. Use eye-catching graphics and short videos to promote your webinars and engage potential attendees. Instagram Stories are particularly effective for creating urgency, allowing you to share countdowns to your webinar date or sneak peeks of what attendees can expect. Collaborating with influencers or other content creators in your niche can also expand your reach, as their followers may be interested in your offerings. Consistent branding across both platforms will help reinforce your message and create a recognizable identity for your webinars.

Content repurposing is an effective strategy to maximize your efforts on Facebook and Instagram. Create short clips or quotes from your webinar and share them as posts or stories to generate interest. This not only provides value to your audience but also encourages them to register for the full webinar to gain deeper insights. Moreover, consider hosting live Q&A sessions on Facebook or Instagram Live to interact directly with your audience. This engagement can build anticipation for your upcoming webinars and encourage immediate sign-ups, as participants can experience firsthand the value you provide.

Analyzing the performance of your social media campaigns is critical for ongoing success. Utilize Facebook Insights and Instagram Analytics to track metrics such as engagement rates, click-through rates, and conversions. These insights can inform your future content strategy and help you adjust your approach based on what resonates with your audience. Understanding which types of posts drive the most traffic to your webinars can refine your promotional efforts, ensuring that you are optimizing your resources for maximum impact. By effectively utilizing Facebook and Instagram, you can create a robust traffic source for your passive income webinars, aligning perfectly with the Lazy Webinar method.

Engaging with LinkedIn Communities

Engaging with LinkedIn communities can significantly enhance your reach and effectiveness in promoting automated webinars. LinkedIn, due to its professional focus, provides a unique platform for connecting with like-minded individuals and potential customers interested in passive income strategies. By actively participating in groups related to your niche, you not only establish your authority but also gain insights into the challenges and needs of your target audience. This allows you to tailor your content and approach to better resonate with potential leads.

When you join relevant LinkedIn groups, take the time to observe the discussions before diving in. Understanding the dynamics of the community will help you determine how best to contribute. Look for common questions or pain points that group members express. By addressing these issues in your posts, you can position yourself as a knowledgeable resource. Sharing valuable content, such as blog articles or video snippets from your webinars, can spark interest and engagement, encouraging members to learn more about your offerings.

Creating meaningful relationships within these communities is essential. Engage with members by commenting on their posts, asking questions, and providing constructive feedback. This interaction not only increases your visibility but also fosters trust and rapport. Once you've established a connection, you can naturally introduce your automated webinar solutions as a means to address their specific needs. Remember, the goal is not to sell directly but to create an environment where your offerings are seen as helpful solutions.

Another effective strategy is to host webinars specifically for the LinkedIn community. These events can be tailored to tackle niche-specific topics that resonate with group members. By providing valuable insights and actionable strategies during the webinar, you enhance your credibility and encourage attendees to explore your passive income methods further. Promote these events within the group and encourage members to invite others who might benefit, expanding your reach and influence.

Finally, it's crucial to analyze the engagement and feedback you receive from your LinkedIn community interactions. Use this data to refine your approach, whether that means adjusting your content strategy or the topics you choose for future webinars. Continuous improvement based on community interactions will not only help you deliver more value but also ensure that your passive profit initiatives remain aligned with the interests of your audience. By leveraging LinkedIn communities effectively, you can create a sustainable pipeline of leads for your automated webinar business.

Running Paid Ads for Webinars

Running paid ads for webinars can significantly enhance your reach and visibility, ensuring that your target audience is aware of your offerings. With the right strategies and platforms, you can drive traffic to your automated webinars and increase your chances of converting leads into customers. The key is to select the appropriate ad channels that align with your audience's preferences and behaviors. Platforms such as Facebook, Google Ads, and LinkedIn can be particularly effective, each offering unique advantages depending on your niche and target demographics.

When creating your paid ad campaigns, it's essential to focus on compelling visuals and messaging that resonate with your audience. Highlight the benefits of attending your webinar, such as exclusive insights, actionable strategies, or expert knowledge. Use clear calls-to-action that encourage users to sign up immediately. A/B testing different ad variations can help determine which combinations of images, headlines, and descriptions yield the best results, allowing you to optimize your advertising efforts continuously.

Retargeting is another powerful strategy to consider when running paid ads for your webinars. By targeting users who have previously engaged with your content or visited your registration page, you can remind them about the value of your webinar and encourage them to complete their registration. This strategy not only increases your conversion rate but also demonstrates your commitment to providing valuable resources tailored to their interests. Implementing retargeting pixels can help track user behavior and streamline your ad campaigns.

Budgeting for paid ads requires careful planning to ensure a positive return on investment. Start with a clear understanding of your cost per acquisition (CPA) and set a budget that allows for adequate testing and scaling. Monitor your campaigns closely, adjusting your bids and targeting based on performance metrics. If certain ads or platforms are generating better results, consider reallocating your budget to maximize effectiveness and enhance overall campaign performance.

Finally, integrating your paid ad efforts with your email marketing automation can create a seamless experience for your audience. Use the data gathered from your ad campaigns to segment your email lists and tailor your messaging accordingly. This approach not only reinforces your webinar promotion but also helps build a relationship with potential attendees, increasing the likelihood of attendance. By combining paid ads with robust email strategies, you can create a comprehensive marketing plan that drives attendance and ultimately leads to passive income through your webinars.

Chapter 10: Crafting Compelling Webinar Scripts

Structuring Your Webinar Narrative

Structuring your webinar narrative is a crucial step in designing an effective presentation that resonates with your audience and drives conversions. A well-structured narrative not only captures attention but also maintains engagement throughout the session. The foundation of a successful webinar narrative begins with understanding your audience's pain points and desires. By addressing their needs directly, you create an emotional connection that encourages participation and investment in your offerings.

The first key element in your narrative structure is a compelling introduction. This section should outline the core problem your audience faces and introduce your solution. By framing the issue in relatable terms, you set the stage for why your webinar is relevant. Use storytelling techniques to draw them in; share a personal anecdote or a case study that exemplifies the challenges they experience. This initial hook is essential for establishing rapport and motivating attendees to stay for the entire presentation.

Following the introduction, the body of your webinar should be segmented into clear, digestible sections. Each segment should build upon the previous one, guiding your audience through a logical progression of information. Incorporate data, testimonials, and case studies to substantiate your claims and enhance credibility. This not only informs but also reassures your audience that your solution is effective. Use visual aids and slides strategically to reinforce key points and keep engagement levels high, ensuring that the information remains accessible.

As you approach the conclusion of your narrative, it is vital to recap the main points and re-emphasize the value of your solution. This is where you can transition into your call to action. Clearly outline what you want your audience to do next, whether it's signing up for a service, making a purchase, or downloading additional resources. Reinforce this call to action by highlighting the benefits they will gain from taking that step. A strong conclusion ties together the entire narrative, leaving attendees with a clear understanding of the next steps and the motivation to act.

Finally, consider the importance of interactivity within your webinar narrative. Encourage questions throughout the presentation and allocate time for a Q&A session at the end. This not only helps address any lingering doubts but also makes your audience feel valued and heard. Incorporating polls or surveys during the webinar can also keep participants engaged and provide insights into their preferences. By structuring your narrative to include interaction, you foster a sense of community and connection, which is essential for converting leads into loyal customers.

Engaging Your Audience

Engaging your audience is a crucial element of the Lazy Webinar Method, as it can significantly impact the effectiveness of your automated presentations. To capture attention from the outset, it's essential to start with a strong hook. This can be a thought-provoking question, an intriguing statistic, or a relatable story that resonates with your target audience. By connecting emotionally and intellectually, you set the stage for a more interactive experience, even in a pre-recorded format. Remember, the goal is to pique curiosity and encourage viewers to stay engaged throughout the entire presentation.

Once you've established that initial connection, maintaining engagement requires a well-structured content delivery. Break your webinar into digestible segments, each focusing on a specific point. Use visuals such as slides, infographics, or video clips to illustrate your message. This not only helps to reinforce key concepts but also caters to various learning styles within your audience. Incorporating questions at the end of each segment encourages reflection and interaction, prompting viewers to think critically about the material presented. This approach enhances retention and fosters a sense of involvement in the learning process.

Incorporating storytelling techniques can also elevate audience engagement. Personal anecdotes or case studies relevant to your niche can help illustrate your points and make the content more relatable. People are naturally drawn to stories, and weaving them into your presentation helps to humanize your message. Additionally, using testimonials or success stories from past participants can build credibility and inspire your audience to envision their own success through your methods. By demonstrating real-world applications of your content, you create a more compelling narrative that captivates viewers.

Utilizing interactive elements can further enhance engagement during your webinars. Though the Lazy Webinar Method is designed for automation, consider incorporating elements such as polls, quizzes, or calls to action that encourage viewers to respond or take immediate steps. These features can be integrated into the webinar platform, allowing for a seamless experience that feels more dynamic. Engaging your audience in this way fosters a sense of community and involvement, making them more likely to act on your recommendations or offers.

Finally, post-webinar engagement is equally important. Following up with attendees through automated email sequences can help reinforce the content, provide additional resources, and encourage feedback. This not only keeps your audience engaged after the presentation but also lays the groundwork for future interactions. By nurturing these relationships and continuing the conversation, you can turn passive viewers into active participants, ultimately driving conversions and enhancing your passive income strategy. Engaging your audience at every stage of the webinar process is essential for maximizing the effectiveness of the Lazy Webinar Method.

Closing the Sale

Closing the sale is a critical phase in the journey of converting leads into loyal customers, especially when utilizing the Lazy Webinar method. This process involves not just presenting your offer but creating a compelling narrative that resonates with your audience's needs and desires. A successful closing strategy hinges on understanding your target market and their pain points, ensuring that your solution is positioned as the ideal answer. By aligning your product or service with their specific challenges, you enhance the likelihood of a conversion, turning interest into action.

To effectively close sales during your automated webinars, it's essential to employ persuasive techniques that encourage immediate action. Incorporating scarcity and urgency can be powerful motivators. Limited-time offers or exclusive bonuses for webinar attendees can spur viewers to make decisions quickly. Communicating the benefits of acting now rather than later can elevate the perceived value of your offer and reduce the chance of procrastination. This strategic framing not only highlights the uniqueness of your offer but also taps into psychological triggers that influence buying behavior.

Another important component of closing the sale is addressing objections proactively. Anticipating common concerns that potential buyers might have allows you to incorporate answers directly into your webinar script. By tackling these objections before they arise, you build trust and credibility with your audience. It's also beneficial to share testimonials or case studies that reinforce the effectiveness of your product, providing social proof that helps alleviate doubts. This evidence can be particularly persuasive in automated settings, where personal interaction is limited.

Utilizing email marketing automation plays a crucial role in reinforcing your closing strategy post-webinar. Following up with attendees through targeted email campaigns keeps your offer fresh in their minds and provides additional opportunities to address any lingering questions they may have. Including personalized messages that reference specific points discussed during the webinar can create a sense of connection and urgency. This follow-up phase is essential for nurturing leads who may not be ready to buy immediately but are interested and may convert later.

Lastly, analyzing webinar metrics after each session is vital for refining your closing techniques. Reviewing data such as viewer engagement rates, drop-off points, and conversion statistics helps identify what resonates with your audience and what doesn't. This continuous improvement process allows you to adjust your content, delivery, and offers to maximize effectiveness. By understanding your audience's behavior and preferences, you can create more compelling narratives and refine your closing strategies, ultimately increasing your passive income potential through the Lazy Webinar method.

Chapter 11: Analyzing Webinar Metrics for Improved Performance

Key Performance Indicators to Track

To effectively measure the success of your lazy webinar approach, it is crucial to establish and monitor key performance indicators (KPIs). These metrics will not only provide insights into your webinar's effectiveness but also guide your strategic adjustments to maximize passive income. Start by tracking the number of registrants, as this figure will give you an initial gauge of interest in your content. The conversion rate from visitor to registrant is also essential, as it reflects the effectiveness of your marketing efforts and the appeal of your webinar topic.

Next, analyze the attendance rate, which is the percentage of registrants who actually participate in the webinar. This KPI highlights potential gaps in your follow-up strategies and can indicate whether your reminder emails are effectively engaging your audience. A low attendance rate may suggest that registrants are losing interest or that the timing of your webinar needs adjustment. Additionally, consider the average watch time during the webinar, as this metric sheds light on how engaged your audience is with the content you present. High engagement often correlates with higher conversion rates for any offers made during the session.

Incorporating post-webinar feedback is another critical KPI. Gather insights through surveys or feedback forms to understand audience reception and the value they found in your presentation. This feedback can guide future content creation and help refine your webinar scripts to better meet the needs of your audience. Furthermore, track the number of leads generated from the webinar. This includes not just immediate sign-ups but also those who might engage with your content in the following days or weeks, demonstrating the ongoing impact of your webinar.

Revenue generated from your automated webinars is perhaps the most crucial KPI. Analyze the relationship between your webinar content, the offers presented, and the sales figures to determine what resonates most with your audience. This metric will help you understand the profitability of your webinars and inform your decisions on future topics and formats. Additionally, consider tracking the customer lifetime value (CLV) of leads generated through your webinars. Understanding how much a customer is worth over time can significantly influence your marketing strategies and budget allocations.

Finally, leverage social media engagement metrics related to your webinar promotions. Monitor shares, likes, and comments to gauge interest and interaction on platforms where your target audience resides. This data can provide insights into how well your promotional efforts are resonating and can guide adjustments to your promotional strategies. By consistently tracking these KPIs, you can refine your lazy webinar method, ensuring it remains a reliable source of passive income while enhancing your automated lead generation strategies.

Interpreting Webinar Data

Webinar data interpretation is crucial for optimizing your automated webinar strategy. By diving deep into the metrics collected during your sessions, you can identify trends, audience behaviors, and key areas for improvement. Start with the foundational statistics such as attendee numbers, registration rates, and live engagement levels. These figures provide insights into how well your promotional efforts are resonating with your target audience. A high registration-to-attendee conversion rate indicates effective marketing, while low numbers may suggest that your messaging or targeting needs refinement.

Next, focus on engagement metrics, such as chat interactions, poll responses, and Q&A participation. These elements are vital in assessing how engaged your audience is during the webinar. A high level of interaction often correlates with greater interest in the content being presented. If engagement is lower than expected, consider revisiting your content delivery methods or examining whether your topics align with your audience's interests. In addition, tracking specific points where attendees drop off can illuminate areas of your presentation that may need to be more compelling or condensed.

Another critical aspect to analyze is conversion data, particularly how many attendees take action after the webinar, whether that means making a purchase, signing up for a newsletter, or engaging with additional content. This metric is essential for understanding the effectiveness of your sales pitch and overall webinar structure. If conversion rates are low, it may be beneficial to experiment with different calls to action or to enhance the urgency of your offers. A/B testing different approaches can provide valuable insights into what resonates most with your audience.

Email marketing automation plays a significant role in nurturing leads generated from your webinars. By examining the response rates to follow-up emails and the sequences of engagement, you can ascertain how well your messages are resonating post-webinar. Metrics such as open rates, click-through rates, and subsequent conversions help you fine-tune your email strategies. Tailoring your email content based on the data collected can significantly increase the effectiveness of your outreach efforts and lead to higher conversion rates.

Finally, integrating social media metrics into your webinar data analysis can enhance your understanding of traffic sources and audience demographics. By tracking social shares, click-through rates from social platforms, and engagement levels, you can assess which channels are most effective for driving webinar traffic. This information allows you to allocate resources towards the most fruitful platforms and tailor your content specifically for those audiences. By continuously interpreting and applying insights from your webinar data, you can refine your strategies to maximize passive income and ensure the long-term success of your automated webinar efforts.

Making Data-Driven Decisions

Making data-driven decisions is essential for optimizing the effectiveness of the Lazy Webinar Method. By leveraging data, webinar creators can identify what resonates with their audience, refine their content, and enhance their marketing strategies. This approach involves analyzing various metrics throughout the webinar process, from lead generation to post-webinar engagement. Data provides insights into audience behavior, preferences, and engagement levels, which can significantly influence the success of automated webinars.

One of the key aspects of making data-driven decisions is tracking engagement metrics during webinars. Metrics such as attendance rates, drop-off points, and interaction levels give creators a clear picture of how well their content is performing. By assessing these statistics, one can determine which segments of the webinar capture the audience's attention and which parts may need refinement. This information is invaluable for crafting high-converting webinar funnels, as it allows creators to tailor their content to meet audience expectations and needs effectively.

In addition to engagement metrics, analyzing lead generation data is crucial for refining automated marketing strategies. By evaluating the sources of leads and their conversion rates, webinar creators can identify the most effective channels for attracting their target audience. This data-driven approach enables them to allocate resources more efficiently, focusing on the strategies that yield the highest return on investment. Whether it's optimizing social media campaigns or adjusting email marketing automation, informed decisions can significantly enhance the overall effectiveness of the Lazy Webinar Method.

Email marketing automation is another critical area where data-driven decisions can lead to improved outcomes. By analyzing open rates, click-through rates, and conversion rates of various email campaigns, creators can identify which messaging resonates most with their audience. This allows for continuous improvement of email marketing strategies, ensuring that promotional materials for webinars effectively engage potential attendees. Personalizing content based on data insights can further enhance engagement, leading to increased attendance and sales.

Lastly, ongoing analysis of webinar performance metrics post-event is vital for long-term success. By examining feedback, surveys, and sales conversion rates after each webinar, creators can make informed adjustments to their future presentations and marketing tactics. This cycle of continuous improvement ensures that each webinar builds upon the successes and challenges of previous ones, ultimately leading to a more refined and profitable automated webinar strategy. In the realm of passive income generation, making data-driven decisions is not just beneficial; it is essential for sustaining growth and maximizing revenue potential.

Chapter 12: Integrating Affiliate Marketing with Automated Webinars

Finding the Right Affiliate Products

Finding the right affiliate products is crucial for maximizing the success of your automated webinars. The products you choose to promote should align closely with the interests and needs of your audience. Start by identifying the specific niche of your webinar topic. Research and select products that not only complement your content but also offer genuine value to your viewers. Whether it's software tools for webinar automation or resources for email marketing, choosing the right products ensures that your audience perceives you as a trusted source of information.

Consider the commission structure and reputation of the affiliate programs you are interested in. High-quality products that provide a strong commission can significantly impact your passive income stream. Investigate the affiliate networks that cater to your niche, as these networks often feature a variety of products to choose from. Look for those that not only offer competitive payouts but also have a good track record of converting leads into sales. This diligence can lead to a more lucrative partnership and enhance the overall credibility of your webinars.

It's also essential to evaluate the promotional materials provided by the affiliate programs. Effective marketing collateral, such as banners, email templates, and social media posts, can save you time and help you create a cohesive marketing strategy. These resources should seamlessly integrate with your existing content, making it easier to promote the products without compromising the overall quality of your webinars. Ensuring that the promotional materials are engaging and aligned with your brand will facilitate a smoother integration of affiliate marketing into your automated webinars.

Another vital aspect is to test the products yourself before promoting them. Authenticity is key in affiliate marketing, and your audience will appreciate your honest opinion. By using the products, you can provide insightful reviews and personal experiences, which can significantly increase your credibility and drive conversions. Sharing case studies or success stories related to the products can further strengthen your position as a knowledgeable authority in your niche.

Lastly, keep an eye on trends and emerging products within your niche. The digital landscape is constantly evolving, and staying updated with the latest tools and resources allows you to adapt your affiliate offerings accordingly. Regularly revisiting your affiliate product selections ensures that you are promoting the best options available. Engaging with your audience through surveys or feedback can also provide insights into what they are interested in, enabling you to refine your product offerings and maximize your passive income potential through the lazy webinar method.

Promoting Affiliates during Your Webinar

Promoting affiliates during your webinar is a strategic approach that can significantly enhance your passive income streams while providing value to your audience. As you prepare your content, consider how affiliate products can complement the topics you are discussing. This not only enriches the experience for your attendees but also opens doors for additional revenue. By integrating affiliate promotions naturally within your webinar, you can maintain the flow of your presentation while subtly guiding your audience toward products that can aid their journey.

One effective method for promoting affiliates is through the use of targeted storytelling. Share personal experiences or case studies that illustrate the benefits of the affiliate products you are endorsing. This narrative technique engages your audience and creates a relatable context, making them more likely to consider the products you recommend. When your audience sees real-life applications of these products, they are not just passive listeners but active participants, which can lead to higher conversion rates.

Incorporating affiliate promotions within your webinar script is crucial. Designate specific portions of your presentation to highlight affiliate products, ensuring that you articulate their value clearly. Use persuasive language that focuses on the problems these products solve or the advantages they offer. Moreover, consider adding visual aids, such as slides or demonstrations, to reinforce the message. This visual engagement can enhance retention and encourage attendees to take action after the webinar concludes.

Another effective strategy is to leverage follow-up emails post-webinar. Automation tools can help you craft personalized messages that include affiliate links and additional resources related to the products discussed during your presentation. This follow-up is vital as it keeps the conversation going and provides attendees with an opportunity to revisit the content. By nurturing this relationship through email marketing automation, you can increase the likelihood of conversions while establishing yourself as a trustworthy resource.

Lastly, measuring the success of your affiliate promotions is essential for long-term growth. Utilize analytics tools to track click-through rates and conversions from your affiliate links. By analyzing this data, you can refine your approach, focusing on the strategies that yield the best results. Continuous improvement based on these metrics not only boosts your affiliate earnings but also enhances the overall quality of your webinars, ensuring they remain valuable and relevant to your audience.

Leveraging Affiliate Relationships for Growth

Leveraging affiliate relationships can significantly amplify your growth when implementing the Lazy Webinar Method. By partnering with affiliates who align with your niche, you can tap into their established audiences, creating a mutually beneficial scenario where both parties can thrive. Affiliates can act as powerful advocates for your automated webinars, promoting your content to their followers while earning commissions on any resulting sales. This approach not only increases your reach but also enhances your credibility, as potential customers are more likely to trust recommendations from influencers they already follow.

To effectively leverage affiliate relationships, it's crucial to identify and select affiliates who resonate with your target audience. Look for individuals or businesses that offer complementary products or services, as they can provide value to your audience and create a seamless experience. Once you have identified potential partners, initiate discussions about collaboration opportunities, outlining how your automated webinars can benefit their audience while also ensuring they understand the commission structure and promotional strategies. This clarity will pave the way for a successful partnership.

Providing affiliates with the right tools and resources is essential for maximizing their promotional efforts. Create a comprehensive affiliate toolkit that includes promotional banners, email templates, and social media posts tailored to your webinars. This not only makes it easier for affiliates to promote your content but also ensures a consistent brand message across various platforms. Additionally, offering exclusive incentives, such as higher commission rates for top performers or bonuses for reaching specific sales milestones, can motivate affiliates to prioritize your webinars in their marketing strategies.

Tracking the performance of your affiliate relationships is vital for understanding their impact on your growth. Utilize tracking links and analytics tools to monitor the success of each affiliate's efforts, providing insights into which partnerships yield the best results. This data can inform your future marketing strategies and help you identify high-performing affiliates worth investing in further. Regular communication with your affiliates, sharing performance metrics, and offering feedback can strengthen these relationships and encourage ongoing collaboration.

Integrating affiliate marketing with your automated webinars not only drives traffic but also fosters a community around your brand. Encourage affiliates to engage with their audiences by sharing personal stories or experiences related to your webinars, creating a more authentic connection. By cultivating a network of passionate affiliates who genuinely believe in your offerings, you can establish a sustainable growth model that leverages the influence of others while providing value to your audience. This symbiotic relationship can lead to increased passive income and a broader reach for your webinars, ultimately solidifying your position in the market.

Chapter 13: Conclusion and Next Steps

Recap of Key Concepts

In this subchapter, we will recap the key concepts that underpin the "Lazy Webinar" method, emphasizing its potential for generating passive income through automation. This approach allows entrepreneurs to create a self-sustaining income stream by leveraging webinars without the need for constant live presentations. By utilizing a combination of automated lead generation strategies and email marketing automation, individuals can effectively drive traffic to their webinars and convert leads into loyal customers.

One of the foundational elements of the "Lazy Webinar" method is the creation of high-converting webinar funnels. These funnels are designed to guide potential customers through a seamless journey, from initial awareness to final purchase. By focusing on the customer experience and eliminating friction points, entrepreneurs can significantly increase their conversion rates. Understanding how to craft compelling webinar scripts tailored to specific niches is also crucial, as it ensures that the content resonates with the target audience and addresses their pain points.

Content repurposing stands out as a vital strategy within this framework. By repurposing existing content into different formats, creators can extend the reach of their webinars and maximize engagement. This not only saves time but also allows for the creation of multiple touchpoints with the audience. Utilizing various platforms, including social media, to promote webinars is another essential aspect, as it enables entrepreneurs to tap into diverse traffic sources and engage with potential attendees where they are most active.

Analyzing webinar metrics is key to improving performance over time. Metrics such as attendance rates, engagement levels, and conversion statistics provide valuable insights into what works and what doesn't. By regularly reviewing these data points, entrepreneurs can refine their strategies, optimize their scripts, and enhance the overall effectiveness of their webinars. This iterative process is crucial for achieving sustainable results and ensuring that the passive income model remains robust.

Finally, integrating affiliate marketing with automated webinars can further amplify the potential for passive income. By promoting relevant affiliate products or services during the webinar, creators can earn additional revenue streams while providing value to their audience. This synergy between the "Lazy Webinar" method and affiliate marketing creates a powerful combination that not only enhances the overall profitability of the webinars but also fosters trust and authority within the niche. In conclusion, mastering these key concepts is essential for leveraging the full potential of the "Lazy Webinar" method in achieving automated income success.

Developing Your Action Plan

Developing an actionable plan is a critical step in successfully implementing the Lazy Webinar Method for passive income generation. This process starts by clearly defining your objectives. What specific outcomes do you want to achieve through your webinars? Whether it's generating leads, driving sales, or building an email list, having well-defined goals will guide your strategy and help you measure success. It's essential to ensure these goals are specific, measurable, achievable, relevant, and time-bound (SMART), as this framework will provide clarity and direction throughout your campaign.

Once your objectives are established, the next step is to identify your target audience. Understanding who you are speaking to is vital for crafting a compelling message that resonates with potential attendees. Conduct market research to uncover your audience's pain points, interests, and preferences. This information will be instrumental in selecting niche-specific topics for your webinars that attract attendees and engage them effectively. Additionally, consider segmenting your audience to tailor content and marketing approaches that cater to different groups within your niche.

With your audience and objectives in place, you can now outline the content and structure of your webinars. Developing high-converting webinar funnels requires not only engaging content but also a clear flow that guides viewers from introduction to conclusion. Crafting compelling webinar scripts is essential, as they serve as the backbone of your presentation. Focus on delivering value while incorporating storytelling elements that captivate your audience. Additionally, be sure to incorporate elements that encourage interaction, such as polls or Q&A sessions, to keep participants engaged and interested.

Next, it's important to leverage the right tools and software for automation. This includes selecting platforms for webinar hosting, email marketing, and analytics that will streamline your processes. Automation is key to the Lazy Webinar Method, as it allows you to set up your webinars to run with minimal ongoing effort. Research various software options to find those that best fit your needs, focusing on features that facilitate automated lead generation and seamless integration with your email marketing strategies.

Finally, your action plan should include a strategy for promoting your webinars and analyzing their performance. Leveraging social media for traffic generation is crucial; develop a promotional schedule that outlines when and where to share your content. Additionally, after each webinar, take time to analyze the metrics gathered to identify areas for improvement. This could include assessing attendance rates, engagement levels, and conversion metrics, which will provide valuable insights that inform future webinars. By continuously refining your approach based on data-driven insights, you can enhance your overall webinar strategy and achieve sustainable passive income.

Continuing Your Education and Growth

Continuing your education and growth is crucial in the fast-paced world of online business, particularly when implementing the Lazy Webinar Method. This method relies heavily on automation, which means that staying updated on the latest trends, tools, and strategies is essential for maintaining and enhancing your passive income streams. Engaging in ongoing learning can help you refine your automated lead generation strategies, ensuring that your webinars attract a steady flow of interested prospects.

One effective way to continue your education is by enrolling in specialized courses that focus on webinar creation and marketing. Many platforms offer comprehensive training on email marketing automation, high-converting webinar funnels, and content repurposing. By investing time in these courses, you can gain insights into the latest techniques and technologies that can elevate your webinars. Such education not only enhances your skill set but also provides you with valuable resources and tools to implement immediately.

Networking with other professionals in your niche can also contribute significantly to your growth. Joining online communities or attending webinars and conferences allows you to interact with peers who share similar goals. These interactions can lead to the sharing of best practices, innovative ideas, and potential collaborations that can enhance your automated webinar strategy. The connections you make can provide ongoing support, encouragement, and inspiration as you navigate the complexities of online marketing.

In addition to formal education and networking, regularly analyzing your webinar metrics is vital for continued improvement. Understanding what works and what doesn't allows you to make data-driven decisions about your content and marketing strategy. By identifying trends in viewer engagement and conversion rates, you can adjust your approach to better meet the needs of your audience. This not only optimizes your current webinars but also informs future topics and presentation styles that resonate with your target market.

Lastly, leveraging social media to stay informed about industry changes and innovations is an integral aspect of your ongoing growth. Following thought leaders, participating in discussions, and consuming relevant content on platforms like LinkedIn or Twitter can keep you abreast of new tools and techniques in webinar automation. By actively engaging with the wider community, you position yourself to capitalize on emerging trends and integrate them into your own strategies, ultimately enhancing your passive income potential through the Lazy Webinar Method.

Webinar Wizardry: Crafting Engaging Content for the Lazy Presenter

Chapter 1: Understanding the Lazy Webinar Method

The Concept of Lazy Presentations

The concept of lazy presentations revolves around the idea of creating impactful webinar content that requires minimal live interaction while still delivering value to the audience. In a world where time is of the essence and attention spans are dwindling, lazy presentations leverage pre-recorded content, automation, and strategic planning to engage viewers without the need for constant live participation. This approach allows presenters to maximize their reach and effectiveness while minimizing the stress and demands of real-time delivery.

Lazy presentations prioritize quality over quantity. By focusing on well-crafted, pre-recorded segments, presenters can meticulously edit their content to ensure clarity, coherence, and visual appeal. This not only enhances the overall quality of the presentation but also allows for the incorporation of various multimedia elements, such as videos, animations, and graphics, which can capture and retain audience attention more effectively than a live speaker might. The ability to refine content before it reaches the audience ensures that every piece of information is presented in the best possible light.

Another significant aspect of lazy presentations is the strategic use of automation. Tools and platforms that allow for automated email reminders, chatbots for audience interaction, and even AI-driven analysis of viewer engagement can streamline the webinar experience. These automated systems can handle many of the logistical challenges that often accompany live presentations, such as managing questions and feedback. This enables presenters to focus on delivering high-quality content rather than being distracted by technical issues or audience management during the live event.

Additionally, lazy presentations cater to the growing demand for on-demand content consumption. By recording webinars and making them available for playback at any time, presenters tap into a shift in how audiences prefer to engage with content. This flexibility allows viewers to digest information at their own pace, revisit complex topics, and share valuable insights with others. The ability to create evergreen content not only extends the life of the presentation but also contributes to ongoing engagement and interaction with the audience long after the initial event has concluded.

Ultimately, the concept of lazy presentations embodies a more efficient and effective approach to webinar creation and delivery. By embracing pre-recorded content, automation, and on-demand accessibility, presenters can achieve their goals without the pressure of live performance. This method fosters a more relaxed atmosphere for both presenters and audiences, promoting a learning environment that prioritizes engagement and value over the traditional demands of live presentations. As the landscape of digital content continues to evolve, adopting the principles of lazy presentations can position webinar creators at the forefront of innovative and impactful online learning experiences.

Benefits of Pre-Recorded Webinars

Pre-recorded webinars offer a myriad of advantages that can significantly enhance the presentation experience, especially for those who prefer a more relaxed approach to content delivery. One of the primary benefits is the elimination of the pressure associated with live presentations. Presenters can take their time to refine their content, ensuring it is polished and professional. This level of preparation allows for a more confident delivery, which can translate into a more engaging experience for viewers. By removing the necessity of real-time interaction, presenters can focus solely on crafting high-quality content that resonates with their audience.

Another notable advantage of pre-recorded webinars is the flexibility they offer in terms of scheduling and accessibility. Unlike live events, which require participants to be available at specific times, pre-recorded webinars can be accessed at any time. This allows presenters to reach a broader audience, accommodating different time zones and personal schedules. Additionally, viewers can revisit the content whenever they wish, reinforcing learning and allowing them to absorb the material at their own pace. This on-demand aspect is particularly appealing in today's fast-paced environment, where individuals often juggle multiple commitments.

Pre-recorded webinars also facilitate enhanced production quality. Presenters have the opportunity to utilize editing tools to eliminate mistakes, insert visuals, and enhance audio quality, creating a more professional final product. This ability to perfect the presentation not only boosts the credibility of the content but also contributes to a more engaging viewer experience. Well-edited webinars can include dynamic elements such as graphics, animations, and transitions that are much more challenging to incorporate in a live setting. This focus on high production values helps maintain viewer interest and encourages retention of the material presented.

Furthermore, pre-recorded webinars are a cost-effective solution for presenters. By eliminating the need for live event logistics, such as venue rental, travel expenses, and technical support, creators can significantly reduce their overhead costs. This financial efficiency can be redirected toward enhancing the quality of the content itself or invested in marketing efforts to attract a larger audience. In a world where budget constraints are common, the ability to create impactful content without incurring high costs is a compelling reason to embrace pre-recorded formats.

Lastly, the analytics capabilities associated with pre-recorded webinars provide valuable insights into audience engagement and behavior. Presenters can track viewer statistics, such as how long individuals watched the webinar and which sections resonated most. This data is crucial for refining future presentations and understanding audience preferences. With the ability to analyze performance metrics, creators can adapt their strategies to better meet the needs of their audience, ultimately leading to improved content and higher conversion rates. By leveraging these insights, presenters can ensure that their pre-recorded webinars remain relevant and effective in a competitive marketplace.

Overcoming Common Misconceptions

Many individuals harbor misconceptions about webinars, particularly regarding their effectiveness without live presentations. One prevalent belief is that live interaction is essential for audience engagement. While live webinars do allow for real-time interaction, pre-recorded webinars can be equally compelling when crafted with thoughtful content and captivating visuals. The key is to focus on delivering high-quality information that resonates with the audience, ensuring that the content remains engaging regardless of the format.

Another common misconception is that creating engaging content for webinars is a time-consuming and labor-intensive process. In reality, with the right strategies and tools, one can streamline content creation significantly. By leveraging templates, outlines, and automation software, presenters can efficiently develop webinars that capture attention and maintain interest. This approach not only reduces the workload but also allows for a polished final product without the stress associated with live presentations.

Some believe that pre-recorded webinars lack authenticity and personal touch compared to live sessions. However, this perception overlooks the opportunity for presenters to refine their delivery. Pre-recording allows for editing, ensuring that content is precisely tailored to meet audience needs and preferences. Furthermore, presenters can incorporate engaging elements such as storytelling, visuals, and interactive components that foster a connection with viewers, creating a sense of authenticity that resonates just as strongly as a live presentation.

Another misconception is that passive viewers do not engage with pre-recorded content. While it may seem that viewers are less likely to participate when not in a live setting, the opposite can be true.

Well-designed webinars can include interactive features such as polls, quizzes, and calls to action that encourage viewer engagement. By strategically placing these elements throughout the presentation, presenters can create a dynamic experience that keeps the audience involved and invested in the content.

Finally, many assume that successful webinars require extensive technical knowledge. This belief can deter potential presenters from exploring the medium altogether. However, the tools and platforms available today are increasingly user-friendly, designed to accommodate individuals with varying levels of technical expertise. By embracing these tools and focusing on the content rather than the technology, anyone can create an effective and engaging webinar that speaks to their audience without the need for extensive technical skills.

Chapter 2: Identifying Your Audience

Defining Your Target Audience

Defining your target audience is a crucial step in crafting engaging content for your webinars, especially when adopting a lazy presentation method. Understanding who your audience is will help you tailor your content to their needs, interests, and pain points, ensuring that your message resonates. Start by identifying demographic factors such as age, gender, location, and profession. This foundational knowledge will provide insights into the general preferences and expectations of your audience, allowing you to create content that speaks directly to them.

Next, delve deeper into psychographic characteristics, which encompass your audience's values, interests, and lifestyle choices. Consider what motivates them and the challenges they face in their personal or professional lives. By addressing these aspects, you can create a more personalized experience for your viewers. For instance, if your audience consists of busy professionals seeking to enhance their skills, your content should reflect their desire for efficiency and relevance. Engaging your audience on a personal level will foster a connection that encourages them to invest their time in your webinar.

Conducting thorough market research is essential in defining your target audience. Utilize surveys, interviews, and social media analytics to gather data on potential viewers. Pay attention to trends and discussions within your niche to identify common queries or interests. This information will help you pinpoint specific topics that your audience is eager to learn about. Additionally, analyzing your competitors can provide insights into what works and what doesn't, allowing you to differentiate your content and offer unique value to your audience.

Creating audience personas can be an effective strategy to visualize and understand your target demographic. These fictional representations should embody the key traits and behaviors of your ideal viewers. By developing personas based on your research, you can create content that speaks directly to their needs and preferences. Consider factors such as their goals, obstacles, and the type of content they consume. This approach will guide your content creation process, ensuring that you remain focused on delivering value that resonates with your audience.

Finally, remember that defining your target audience is an ongoing process. As trends evolve and new information emerges, continuously reassess your understanding of your audience. Solicit feedback after each webinar and analyze engagement metrics to refine your approach. Staying attuned to your audience's changing preferences will not only enhance the relevance of your content but also help you maintain a loyal viewership. By focusing on your audience's needs and preferences, you can create engaging webinars that achieve your desired outcomes while embracing a more relaxed presentation style.

Understanding Audience Pain Points

Identifying and addressing audience pain points is crucial for creating engaging webinar content, particularly when the goal is to captivate a passive audience. Pain points refer to the specific problems, challenges, or frustrations that your audience faces. By understanding these issues, you can tailor your content to meet their needs, making the webinar more relevant and impactful. This involves conducting thorough research to uncover the common struggles within your niche, whether through surveys, social media interactions, or industry forums.

Once you have identified the pain points, it is essential to categorize them into different types. Pain points can generally be classified into four categories: financial, productivity, process, and emotional. Financial pain points often relate to cost-saving measures or budget constraints. Productivity pain points revolve around time management and efficiency. Process pain points typically involve the complexities and inefficiencies of existing systems. Emotional pain points may stem from frustration, fear, or anxiety related to their situation. Recognizing which category your audience's pain points fall into can guide the development of your content strategy.

Incorporating the identified pain points into your webinar content not only enhances relevance but also fosters a deeper connection with your audience. When participants see that you understand their struggles, they are more likely to engage with the material. Start by addressing these pain points early in the presentation. Use storytelling techniques to illustrate common scenarios that your audience may face, thereby creating an emotional resonance that captures their attention. This approach makes your content relatable and encourages viewers to reflect on their own experiences.

Moreover, it is vital to provide actionable solutions to the pain points you've highlighted. Your audience will attend your webinar in search of answers, so presenting clear, practical strategies and tips is essential. For instance, if a common pain point is the difficulty in creating engaging content, offer step-by-step guidance on how to structure a webinar or utilize visual aids effectively. By equipping your audience with tools and techniques to overcome their challenges, you not only position yourself as an expert but also build trust and credibility.

Finally, continuous feedback is key to understanding whether you have successfully addressed your audience's pain points. After the webinar, solicit feedback through surveys or direct communication. This will not only provide insight into what resonated with your audience but also highlight any additional pain points you may have overlooked. By iterating on your content based on this feedback, you can continually refine your webinars to ensure that they remain engaging and relevant, ultimately enhancing the overall experience for your viewers.

Tailoring Content for Maximum Engagement

Tailoring content for maximum engagement is essential for creating webinars that resonate with an audience, especially when live presentations are not an option. Understanding the audience's preferences, needs, and pain points allows presenters to craft messages that speak directly to them. By conducting thorough research on the target demographic, including their interests and challenges, content creators can develop a narrative that aligns with the audience's expectations. This foundational knowledge sets the stage for building engaging content that keeps viewers invested.

Once the audience insights are gathered, the next step is to structure the content in a way that maintains interest throughout the presentation. Utilizing storytelling techniques can significantly enhance engagement. A compelling story can create an emotional connection, making the information more relatable and memorable. Presenters should aim to weave personal anecdotes, case studies, or hypothetical scenarios into the material, allowing the audience to visualize the concepts being discussed. This method fosters a sense of involvement, drawing viewers into the narrative and encouraging them to reflect on their experiences.

In addition to storytelling, incorporating interactive elements is crucial for maintaining engagement in a webinar format. Tools like polls, quizzes, and question prompts can break up the presentation and invite participation, even in a recorded format. These elements not only provide a momentary distraction from passive viewing but also encourage the audience to engage actively with the content. By prompting viewers to think critically about the material and respond, presenters can create a dynamic experience that reduces the likelihood of disengagement.

Visual aids also play a significant role in tailoring content for engagement. Well-designed slides, infographics, and videos can enhance understanding and retention of information. It is important for presenters to ensure that visual elements directly support the spoken content rather than overwhelm it. Striking a balance between informative visuals and succinct text allows the audience to focus on the key messages without feeling overwhelmed. The use of color, typography, and imagery should be carefully considered to create a cohesive and appealing presentation that captures attention.

Finally, effective closing strategies can leave a lasting impact on the audience. Summarizing key points and providing actionable takeaways reinforce the value of the content presented. Encouraging viewers to implement what they have learned and offering additional resources can foster a sense of community and support. By inviting feedback or questions, presenters can also extend the engagement beyond the webinar itself, nurturing ongoing interaction and interest. This approach not only enhances the immediate experience but also lays the groundwork for future connections and opportunities.

Chapter 3: Crafting Compelling Webinar Content

Structuring Your Webinar for Impact

Structuring your webinar for impact is essential to ensure that your audience not only retains the information presented but also feels compelled to take action afterward. The first step in this process is to clearly define your objectives. Determine what you want your attendees to learn and the desired outcomes you hope to achieve. This clarity will guide your content creation and ensure that every element of your webinar serves a purpose. Consider the specific problems your audience faces and how your content can provide solutions. By aligning your objectives with your audience's needs, you can create a focused and impactful webinar.

Once your objectives are established, the next step is to develop a clear and logical flow for your presentation. A well-structured webinar typically follows a format that includes an engaging introduction, informative body, and persuasive conclusion. Start with an introduction that captures attention, outlines the topics to be covered, and establishes your credibility. This can be achieved through storytelling or presenting a surprising statistic relevant to your audience. Transition smoothly into the body of the presentation, breaking down complex information into digestible segments. Utilize bullet points or numbered lists to highlight key ideas, making it easier for viewers to follow along.

Incorporating multimedia elements can significantly enhance the impact of your webinar. Visual aids such as slides, infographics, and videos can help reinforce your message and maintain audience engagement. Ensure that these elements are high quality and relevant to the content being presented. Additionally, consider using interactive features such as polls, quizzes, or Q&A sessions, even in a pre-recorded format. These interactive components encourage participation and create a more dynamic experience for viewers, making them feel more connected to the content.

Keep in mind the importance of pacing throughout your webinar. A well-paced presentation allows the audience to absorb information without feeling overwhelmed. Aim for a rhythm that balances information delivery with pauses for reflection and engagement. Avoid the temptation to rush through your material; instead, allow time for key points to resonate with your audience. A good rule of thumb is to allocate time for each section of your presentation and stick to it, ensuring that you cover all intended content without exceeding your time limit.

Finally, conclude your webinar with a strong closing that reinforces the key messages delivered. Summarize the main points and reiterate how they address the challenges faced by your audience. This is also the opportunity to provide a clear call to action, guiding attendees on the next steps they should take after the presentation. Whether it's signing up for a newsletter, accessing additional resources, or making a purchase, a well-defined call to action can significantly increase engagement. By thoughtfully structuring your webinar, you create a compelling experience that leaves a lasting impression on your audience and drives them towards the desired outcomes.

The Art of Storytelling in Webinars

The art of storytelling in webinars transforms a simple presentation into a compelling narrative that captivates the audience. Unlike traditional lectures that often rely on data and statistics, storytelling creates an emotional connection that enhances engagement. By weaving personal anecdotes, case studies, or relatable scenarios into the content, presenters can draw listeners in, making complex concepts more digestible. This narrative approach not only keeps the audience interested but also fosters a deeper understanding of the material being presented.

Effective storytelling in webinars often follows a structured format that includes a beginning, middle, and end. The beginning introduces the main theme or problem, creating a sense of curiosity or urgency. This can be achieved by presenting a relatable challenge that the audience might face. The middle of the narrative should explore the journey to finding solutions, illustrating the challenges encountered along the way. This part can include testimonials or success stories that resonate with the audience, allowing them to visualize their own potential transformation. Finally, the end should wrap up the story by presenting a resolution or takeaway that encourages action, reinforcing the core message of the webinar.

Incorporating visuals can significantly enhance the storytelling experience in webinars. Visual aids such as slides, infographics, and videos can complement the narrative by providing context and reinforcing key points. A well-designed slide deck can serve as a visual narrative that aligns with the spoken word, making it easier for the audience to follow along. Additionally, incorporating multimedia elements can evoke emotions, creating a richer experience that holds attention and encourages retention of information.

Another crucial aspect of storytelling in webinars is the use of language and tone. Presenters should strive to adopt a conversational style that invites participation and engagement. This approach makes the audience feel as though they are part of a dialogue rather than passive recipients of information. Using metaphors, analogies, and vivid descriptions can help paint a picture in the audience's mind, making the content more relatable and impactful. The choice of words should resonate with the target audience, ensuring that the message is both accessible and appealing.

Lastly, practice and refinement of storytelling techniques are essential for success in webinars. Presenters should consider rehearsing their narratives to ensure smooth delivery and timing. Gathering feedback from test audiences can provide valuable insights into what resonates and what may need adjustment. By continuously refining their storytelling skills, presenters can enhance their effectiveness in engaging the audience, ultimately leading to a more impactful webinar experience. Emphasizing the art of storytelling not only enriches the content but also empowers presenters to connect with their audience on a deeper level, making each webinar a memorable event.

Utilizing Visuals and Multimedia Effectively

Utilizing visuals and multimedia effectively is crucial in creating engaging webinar content, especially when aiming for a passive audience. Visuals, such as images, infographics, and charts, serve to break up text-heavy slides and keep viewers interested. They can illustrate complex ideas quickly and concisely, allowing for easier comprehension. For instance, a well-designed infographic can encapsulate a series of statistics in a way that is not only visually appealing but also immediately informative. This helps maintain attention and reinforces the key messages being delivered.

Incorporating video elements can further enhance the viewer's experience. Pre-recorded video clips can serve to introduce topics, provide testimonials, or showcase product demonstrations. These dynamic elements can evoke emotional responses and create a sense of connection, even in a passive format. By strategically placing these video segments throughout the webinar, presenters can create natural breaks in the content that allow for information absorption without overwhelming the audience.

Sound effects and background music are additional layers that can elevate the overall presentation. Appropriate audio can set the mood and tone of the webinar, guiding the audience's emotional journey through the content. For example, a subtle background track can create a relaxed atmosphere, while more upbeat music can energize viewers during key moments. However, it is imperative to use audio judiciously; overwhelming soundscapes can distract rather than enhance, so a careful balance must be struck.

Interactive elements, such as polls and quizzes, are another effective way to engage participants, even in a pre-recorded format. These features can prompt viewers to reflect on the material and encourage them to interact with the content actively. By embedding occasional questions or polls throughout the presentation, the audience feels involved, fostering a sense of participation and investment in the material being shared.

Lastly, accessibility should never be overlooked. Ensuring that visuals and multimedia are accessible to all potential viewers is essential. This includes providing captions for videos, alt text for images, and considering color contrast for those with visual impairments. By prioritizing accessibility, presenters not only adhere to best practices but also expand their audience reach, making the content available to a broader spectrum of learners. In a world where inclusivity is increasingly important, taking these steps can enhance the overall effectiveness of a webinar while showcasing a commitment to audience engagement.

Chapter 4: Tools and Technologies for Lazy Presenters

Choosing the Right Webinar Platform

Choosing the right webinar platform is a critical step in ensuring the success of your online presentations, especially when catering to an audience that prefers to engage without the pressures of live presentations. The ideal platform should align with your content delivery style and technical requirements. Start by assessing the specific features that different platforms offer, such as ease of use, customization options, and integration capabilities with other tools. Look for platforms that allow you to create pre-recorded webinars, as this aligns perfectly with the lazy presenter approach.

Another important consideration is audience capacity. Depending on the size of your target audience, you need a platform that can handle the number of participants you expect. Some platforms are better suited for smaller, intimate sessions, while others can accommodate large groups without compromising performance. Additionally, take into account the quality of video and audio streaming, as well as the platform's reliability during playback. A seamless experience is crucial for maintaining viewer engagement and ensuring that your content is delivered effectively.

User experience plays a significant role in your choice of webinar platform. Look for platforms that offer an intuitive interface for both presenters and participants. This includes easy navigation, clear instructions, and accessible features like chat and Q&A options. A user-friendly platform can minimize technical difficulties, allowing you to focus on delivering your content rather than troubleshooting issues. Consider testing a few platforms with trial versions to gauge how comfortable you feel using each one and how well they cater to your audience's needs.

Integration with marketing and automation tools is another key factor in selecting a webinar platform. The ability to connect with email marketing services, CRM systems, and social media channels can enhance your promotional efforts and streamline the registration process. Look for platforms that provide analytics and reporting features, allowing you to track engagement metrics and audience behavior. These insights can help you refine your content strategy and optimize future webinars, making your presentations not only more engaging but also more effective in driving conversions.

Finally, consider the cost of the webinar platform and how it fits into your overall budget. While some platforms offer free versions, they may lack essential features that are necessary for a polished presentation. Weigh the benefits of premium options against your specific needs to find the best value. Remember that investing in a reliable platform can pay off in terms of increased audience engagement and satisfaction, ultimately leading to better results for your passive profit ventures. By carefully evaluating these factors, you can choose a webinar platform that enhances your lazy presenter strategy and helps you create compelling, engaging content.

Essential Recording and Editing Tools

When it comes to creating engaging webinar content without live presentations, having the right recording and editing tools is essential. These tools not only streamline the production process but also enhance the overall quality of your webinars. A combination of hardware and software can make a significant difference in how your content is perceived. High-quality audio and video equipment, along with user-friendly editing software, are fundamental elements in producing professional-grade webinars that captivate your audience.

For recording, a good microphone is crucial. Clear audio is often more important than video quality, as poor sound can quickly disengage viewers. Consider investing in a USB condenser microphone, which offers excellent sound clarity and is easy to set up. Additionally, a high-definition webcam or a DSLR camera can elevate your video quality. When recording, ensure your environment is quiet and well-lit to minimize distractions and enhance the viewer experience. Using a green screen can also provide a polished background, allowing you to present your content in a visually appealing manner.

Editing software plays a pivotal role in refining your recorded content. Programs like Camtasia, Adobe Premiere Pro, or Final Cut Pro offer robust features for trimming, adding text overlays, and incorporating transitions. For those who prefer simpler solutions, tools like iMovie or Filmora can provide sufficient editing capabilities without overwhelming complexity. It's important to familiarize yourself with the software you choose, as mastering its features can significantly improve the pacing and flow of your webinars. Learning to edit effectively will enable you to create a seamless viewing experience, keeping your audience engaged from start to finish.

Incorporating additional tools can further enhance your webinar production. Screen recording software like OBS Studio or Snagit allows you to capture presentations or demonstrations directly from your screen, making it easier to showcase slides or software in action. Additionally, having access to a library of royalty-free music and sound effects can add depth to your webinars, making them more dynamic and enjoyable. Be mindful of licensing requirements when using external content, as adhering to copyright laws is crucial in maintaining your professionalism.

Lastly, don't underestimate the importance of post-production processes. Once your webinar is recorded and edited, consider using tools for video compression and optimization to ensure smooth playback across various devices and platforms. Platforms like HandBrake can help reduce file sizes without sacrificing quality. Engaging thumbnails and compelling descriptions are also vital for attracting viewers to your content. By investing time and resources into these essential recording and editing tools, you can create webinars that not only convey your message effectively but also resonate with your audience, ultimately leading to greater engagement and success in your passive profit endeavors.

Automation Tools for Engagement

Automation tools play a crucial role in enhancing engagement for webinars, particularly for presenters who prefer a more passive approach. These tools streamline various aspects of the webinar process, allowing creators to focus on content quality rather than the mechanics of delivery. By incorporating automation, presenters can effectively maintain audience interest and interaction, even in the absence of live presentations. This chapter explores various automation tools designed specifically for engaging webinar content, ensuring that presenters maximize their reach and impact.

One of the most valuable types of automation tools is email marketing software. These platforms allow presenters to create automated email sequences that nurture leads before, during, and after the webinar. By sending out a series of well-timed emails, presenters can build anticipation, provide reminders, and follow up with additional resources or calls to action. Email marketing tools also enable segmentation, allowing presenters to tailor messages based on audience interests or behaviors, which can significantly enhance engagement rates.

Another essential category of automation tools includes webinar platforms that offer features such as pre-recorded sessions, interactive polls, and automated Q&A sessions. These platforms allow presenters to record their content in advance, ensuring that the quality of delivery is polished and professional. Additionally, features like polls and Q&A can be automated to create an interactive experience that mimics live engagement. This functionality encourages viewers to participate actively, providing valuable feedback and insights that can be leveraged for future presentations.

Social media automation tools also play a vital role in promoting webinars and engaging potential attendees. These tools help presenters schedule and distribute content across various social media channels, generating buzz and attracting a larger audience. By automating posts, presenters can maintain a consistent online presence without the need for constant manual updates. Additionally, using analytics from these platforms can help presenters gauge audience interest and adapt their content strategy accordingly, ultimately leading to higher engagement.

Finally, leveraging customer relationship management (CRM) systems can significantly enhance engagement by tracking interactions and personalizing outreach. CRMs can automate follow-up emails based on user behavior and engagement metrics, ensuring that the right messages reach the right audience at the right time. This personalization fosters a deeper connection with viewers, making them feel valued and understood. By integrating these automation tools into their webinar strategy, presenters can create a seamless and engaging experience that resonates with participants, ultimately driving better results.

Chapter 5: Designing Your Webinar

Creating Captivating Slides

Creating captivating slides is essential for enhancing engagement in webinars, especially when presenters seek to deliver compelling content without the need for live presentations. The foundation of effective slides lies in their ability to complement the spoken word rather than distract from it. To achieve this balance, presenters should focus on a clear and concise design that reinforces key messages, ensuring that the audience remains attentive and retains the information presented.

One of the critical elements in slide design is simplicity. Each slide should communicate a single idea or concept, preventing cognitive overload for viewers. Using minimal text and incorporating visuals, such as images or infographics, can significantly enhance understanding. When slides are cluttered with excessive information or complex graphics, the audience may struggle to grasp the message, leading to disengagement. By adhering to the principle of "less is more," presenters can create slides that are both visually appealing and informative.

Color and font choices also play a significant role in the effectiveness of webinar slides. Selecting a color palette that is visually harmonious can help maintain a professional appearance while also emphasizing important points. Additionally, utilizing legible fonts that are consistent throughout the presentation ensures that viewers can easily read the content. It is advisable to use larger font sizes for headlines and key points, while maintaining smaller sizes for supplementary information. This hierarchy guides viewers' attention and allows them to follow along seamlessly.

Incorporating multimedia elements can further enhance the impact of slides. Short video clips, animations, or audio snippets can provide a break from static images and engage the audience on a different sensory level. However, it is crucial to ensure that these elements are directly relevant to the content and serve a clear purpose. Overusing multimedia can lead to distraction, so it is essential to strike a balance that keeps the focus on the main message while adding value to the overall presentation.

Finally, practicing the delivery of the presentation alongside the slides is vital for achieving a cohesive experience. Familiarity with the slide content allows presenters to speak confidently and fluidly, ensuring that the audience remains engaged throughout. It is also beneficial to gather feedback from peers or conduct dry runs to identify areas for improvement. By continuously refining their approach, presenters can create captivating slides that not only attract attention but also enhance the overall effectiveness of their webinars, ultimately leading to a more successful passive profit strategy.

Incorporating Interactive Elements

Incorporating interactive elements into webinars is essential for maintaining audience engagement, especially when the format leans towards pre-recorded content. These elements can transform a passive viewing experience into an interactive learning journey, helping to create a stronger connection between the presenter and the audience. Various tools and strategies can be utilized to achieve this, ensuring that participants feel involved and valued throughout the session.

One effective way to incorporate interactivity is through polls and surveys. By strategically placing these elements at key moments during the presentation, presenters can solicit immediate feedback or opinions from their audience. This not only breaks up the content but also provides valuable insights into audience preferences and understanding. Utilizing live polling tools allows participants to express their views in real time, offering a sense of participation that can energize the session and keep attention focused.

Another approach to fostering interactivity is through quizzes and gamification. Including short quizzes related to the content can reinforce learning and retention while making the experience enjoyable. Gamification elements, such as leaderboards or rewards for participation, can motivate attendees to engage more actively. This not only enhances their learning experience but also encourages them to invest their time and effort in the webinar content, leading to better outcomes for both the audience and the presenter.

Incorporating interactive Q&A sessions is another powerful strategy. Even in a pre-recorded format, presenters can invite questions in advance or during specific segments of the webinar. Addressing these questions directly in the presentation allows for a more personalized experience and demonstrates that the presenter values audience input. This interaction can help clarify complex topics and foster a sense of community among participants, as they see their concerns and queries being acknowledged.

Lastly, utilizing social media or community forums to extend the interaction beyond the webinar itself can create lasting engagement. Encouraging attendees to share their thoughts, insights, or questions on social platforms can foster a vibrant community atmosphere. This ongoing dialogue not only keeps the conversation alive but also creates opportunities for attendees to network and collaborate, enhancing the overall value of the experience. By incorporating these interactive elements, presenters can craft webinars that resonate deeply with their audience, ultimately leading to a more memorable and impactful learning experience.

Ensuring Accessibility for All Viewers

Ensuring accessibility for all viewers is a crucial aspect of crafting engaging webinar content. As you design your presentations, consider the diverse backgrounds, abilities, and technological capacities of your audience. Accessibility means more than just meeting legal requirements; it involves creating an inclusive environment where everyone can participate fully. This approach not only demonstrates your commitment to inclusivity but also broadens your audience base, allowing more people to benefit from your insights.

One of the first steps in ensuring accessibility is to provide captions and transcripts for your webinars. These tools assist viewers who are deaf or hard of hearing, as well as those who may have difficulty understanding spoken language due to various reasons. By integrating real-time captioning or providing a transcript after the session, you cater to these groups and enhance the experience for all participants. Additionally, captions can help non-native speakers follow along more easily, thereby expanding your reach even further.

Another critical consideration is the visual design of your content. Use high-contrast colors to ensure that text is easily readable against the background. Avoid using color combinations that are challenging for those with color blindness, such as green and red. Moreover, use clear fonts and maintain a consistent style throughout your presentation. When incorporating visuals, provide descriptive alt text for images and graphics. This practice allows screen readers to convey the content to visually impaired users, ensuring that no one misses out on important information.

Interactive elements in webinars can greatly enhance engagement, but they must also be accessible. Ensure that polls, quizzes, and other interactive tools are designed with accessibility in mind. For example, provide keyboard navigation options and ensure that all interactive features can be used with assistive technologies. This attention to detail not only makes your content more engaging but also ensures that all participants can interact with the material in a meaningful way.

Finally, consider the platform you choose for hosting your webinars. Some platforms offer better accessibility features than others, such as screen reader compatibility, keyboard navigation, and customizable interfaces. Research and select a platform that prioritizes accessibility, as this decision will directly impact the experience of your viewers. By taking these steps to ensure accessibility, you create a welcoming environment where everyone can engage with your content effectively, allowing you to master the lazy webinar method while promoting inclusion and maximizing your audience potential.

Chapter 6: Pre-Recording Your Webinar

Best Practices for Recording

When it comes to recording webinars, best practices can significantly enhance the overall quality and engagement of your content. First and foremost, invest in a good microphone and camera. Audio quality is often more important than video quality, as poor sound can lead to viewer frustration and disengagement. A clear, crisp audio experience helps to convey authority and professionalism. Similarly, using a high-definition camera can elevate your visual presence, making your content more appealing. Ensure your recording environment is quiet and well-lit, as this will further enhance the viewer's experience.

Next, consider your script and presentation materials carefully. Even though you may not be presenting live, a well-structured script is crucial for maintaining a smooth flow of information. Outline your main points and practice delivering them in a conversational tone. This approach will help you sound more natural and engaging, even when recorded. Accompany your narration with visually stimulating slides or graphics that reinforce your message. Avoid cluttered slides; instead, focus on key visuals that complement your spoken words to keep your audience's attention.

Editing plays a vital role in the final quality of your recorded webinars. Invest time in post-production to cut out unnecessary pauses, filler words, or mistakes. Also, consider adding background music or sound effects to enhance emotional engagement, but ensure they are subtle and do not overpower your voice. Use editing software to include text overlays for key points or statistics, which can help reinforce your message visually. A well-edited webinar can transform a good presentation into a great one, making it more enjoyable for viewers.

Another important aspect is to create engaging content through storytelling. Rather than just presenting facts, weave narratives that resonate with your audience. Use case studies, examples, or personal anecdotes to illustrate your points. This technique not only makes the content more relatable but also helps in retaining viewer interest. When viewers can connect emotionally with your content, they are more likely to engage with it and retain the information presented.

Lastly, remember to promote interaction, even in a recorded format. Encourage viewers to comment, ask questions, or share their own experiences in the comments section or through follow-up emails. Consider incorporating polls or quizzes during the webinar that viewers can respond to after watching. This not only enhances engagement but also provides you with valuable feedback for future webinars. By following these best practices for recording, you can create compelling webinar content that resonates deeply with your audience, ensuring that your message is heard and remembered.

Tips for a Professional Presentation

When preparing for a professional presentation, clarity of message is paramount. Start by defining the key points you want to communicate. Aim for a clear structure that guides your audience through your content. Each segment should build on the previous one, reinforcing your overall message. Break down complex ideas into digestible parts, ensuring that your audience can easily follow along. Use simple language and avoid jargon unless it is widely understood within your niche. This approach not only enhances comprehension but also keeps your audience engaged.

Visual aids can significantly enhance your presentation. Use slides, infographics, or videos to complement your spoken content and provide visual interest. Ensure that these materials are high-quality and relevant to the topic. Each visual should serve a purpose, whether it is to illustrate a point, provide evidence, or evoke an emotional response. Avoid overcrowding slides with text; instead, use bullet points and images to convey information succinctly. This allows your audience to focus on your spoken words while still having a visual reference to reinforce your message.

Practice is essential for delivering a professional presentation. Rehearse multiple times to become familiar with your content and the flow of your presentation. This will help you identify any areas that may need clarification or adjustment. Record yourself during practice sessions to evaluate your pacing, tone, and body language. Pay attention to how you convey confidence and enthusiasm, as these traits are infectious and can significantly impact audience engagement. The more comfortable you are with your material, the more effectively you can connect with your audience.

Engagement techniques can transform a standard presentation into an interactive experience. Consider incorporating polls, quizzes, or Q&A segments to involve your audience actively. Even in a pre-recorded format, you can encourage participation by inviting viewers to comment or share their thoughts during the presentation. This engagement not only keeps the audience interested but also creates a sense of community among participants. Remember to acknowledge their contributions, as this fosters a positive atmosphere and encourages further interaction.

Finally, conclude your presentation effectively. Summarize your key points and reiterate the main message to reinforce what you've shared. Provide a clear call to action, whether it's prompting the audience to implement what they've learned, visit your website, or engage with additional resources. A strong conclusion leaves a lasting impression and encourages your audience to reflect on the content long after the presentation ends. By following these tips, you can deliver a professional presentation that captivates and informs, making a lasting impact on your audience.

Editing Your Webinar for Clarity

Editing your webinar for clarity is a crucial step that can significantly enhance the effectiveness of your presentation. The goal is to ensure that your audience can easily grasp the key concepts and ideas being communicated. Start by reviewing the entire content to identify sections that may be confusing or overly complex. The language used should be straightforward, avoiding jargon or technical terms unless they are essential to the topic. When editing, ask yourself if each section serves a clear purpose and contributes to the overall message of the webinar.

One effective technique for improving clarity is to break down complex ideas into simpler components. This can be achieved through the use of analogies, examples, or visuals that make the information more digestible. If a particular segment feels dense or overwhelming, consider restructuring it into smaller parts. Each part should build on the previous one, creating a logical flow that guides the audience through the material. This approach not only aids understanding but also keeps viewers engaged by providing them with manageable chunks of information.

Another critical aspect of editing is to eliminate redundancy. Repetition can dilute your message and cause audience fatigue. Go through your content and remove any repetitive statements or ideas. Instead, focus on reinforcing key points in a concise manner. This can be done by summarizing important concepts at the end of each section, which helps reinforce the material without unnecessary repetition. A well-edited webinar should feel streamlined, with each point adding value to the overall narrative.

Incorporating feedback from others can also enhance clarity. Share your edited webinar with a trusted colleague or mentor who can provide an outside perspective. They may identify areas that are still unclear or suggest alternative phrasing that may resonate better with the intended audience. This collaborative approach can uncover blind spots and lead to improvements that you might not have considered on your own. It's essential to be open to constructive criticism, as it can provide valuable insights into how your content is perceived.

Finally, consider the pacing of your webinar. Rapid-fire delivery can overwhelm viewers, while a sluggish pace can lead to disengagement. As you edit, think about how long each section takes to present and adjust accordingly. Use pauses effectively to allow your audience to absorb key points, and ensure that transitions between sections are smooth and logical. A well-paced presentation not only enhances clarity but also contributes to a more enjoyable viewing experience, making it easier for your audience to retain the information presented.

Chapter 7: Promoting Your Webinar

Building a Landing Page That Converts

Building a landing page that converts is a critical component of any successful webinar strategy, especially for those seeking to engage an audience without live presentations. A well-designed landing page serves as the first impression for potential attendees, and it must convey the value of the webinar succinctly and compellingly. To achieve this, it is essential to focus on clarity and purpose. The headline should immediately capture attention, presenting a clear benefit or solution that resonates with the target audience. This sets the stage for the rest of the page, guiding visitors toward taking action.

Incorporating persuasive elements is vital in enhancing conversion rates. Utilizing bullet points to outline key takeaways from the webinar can effectively highlight the value proposition. This not only makes it easier for visitors to digest the information but also emphasizes the specific outcomes they can expect. Alongside this, including testimonials or social proof can bolster credibility. Potential attendees are more likely to register if they see that others have benefited from similar content. Therefore, strategically placed testimonials can make a significant difference in how visitors perceive the value of the webinar.

Visual design plays an equally important role in creating a landing page that converts. A clean, professional layout with an attractive color scheme can enhance user experience. Images or graphics that support the webinar's theme can capture attention and maintain interest. It is important to ensure that visuals do not overwhelm the text but rather complement it. Additionally, employing a clear call-to-action (CTA) is essential. The CTA should be prominent and compelling, guiding visitors to register for the webinar with minimal friction. Phrases like "Reserve Your Spot Now" or "Join Us for Exclusive Insights" can create a sense of urgency.

Another crucial aspect of a high-converting landing page is mobile optimization. With an increasing number of users accessing content via mobile devices, ensuring that the landing page is responsive is imperative. A mobile-friendly design not only improves user experience but also impacts conversion rates positively. This means that all elements, from images to CTAs, should function seamlessly on smaller screens. Testing the page across different devices and browsers can help identify any issues that may hinder the registration process.

Finally, ongoing optimization and testing of the landing page can significantly enhance its effectiveness. Utilizing A/B testing allows marketers to experiment with different headlines, images, and CTAs to determine which combinations yield the highest conversions. Analyzing user behavior through tools like heatmaps can provide insights into how visitors interact with the page. This data can inform adjustments and improvements, ensuring that the landing page remains relevant and effective in attracting and converting potential attendees. By continually refining this essential component of the webinar strategy, presenters can maximize their outreach and impact, even without live presentations.

Utilizing Social Media for Promotion

Utilizing social media for promotion is essential for maximizing the reach and engagement of your webinar content. Social media platforms provide a powerful avenue for promoting your webinars, allowing you to connect with a broader audience and foster a community around your topic. By leveraging platforms such as Facebook, Twitter, LinkedIn, and Instagram, you can create anticipation and excitement about your upcoming webinars. Each platform has its unique characteristics and user demographics, so understanding where your target audience spends their time is key to effective promotion.

One effective strategy is to create visually appealing promotional materials tailored to each platform. For instance, using eye-catching graphics and videos on Instagram can help capture attention, while informative posts on LinkedIn can appeal to a more professional audience. Consider creating short teaser videos or infographics that highlight the key benefits of attending your webinar. These promotional assets should align with your branding and convey a clear message about what participants can expect to learn, thereby enticing them to register.

Engaging with your audience is another critical aspect of utilizing social media. Regularly posting updates, responding to comments, and encouraging discussions can help build a sense of community and keep your audience informed. Use polls, questions, and interactive posts to gauge interest and gather feedback on topics your audience is passionate about. This engagement not only boosts visibility in social media algorithms but also fosters a loyal following that is more likely to attend your webinars.

Incorporating user-generated content can further enhance your promotional efforts. Encourage past participants to share their experiences on social media by tagging your webinar account or using a specific hashtag. This not only provides social proof but also extends your reach as their followers become aware of your content. Sharing testimonials, quotes, or highlights from previous webinars can serve as compelling endorsements, motivating potential attendees to register.

Finally, establishing a consistent posting schedule is crucial for maintaining momentum in your promotional efforts. Use a content calendar to plan and organize your posts leading up to the webinar. This approach ensures that you are consistently reminding your audience about the event while providing valuable content related to the webinar topic. By strategically timing your promotions, you can maximize visibility and engagement, ultimately driving higher registration and attendance rates for your webinars.

Email Marketing Strategies

Email marketing remains a cornerstone strategy for engaging audiences and driving conversions, particularly in the context of webinars. For those mastering the lazy webinar method, leveraging email can effectively nurture leads and keep them informed about upcoming content. The key to successful email marketing lies in creating targeted, relevant, and compelling messages that resonate with your audience. Understanding audience segmentation allows you to tailor your communications based on their interests and behaviors, ensuring that your emails are not just opened but also acted upon.

One effective strategy is to build a pre-webinar email sequence that warms up your audience. Start by sending a series of emails that provide valuable insights related to your webinar topic. This could include tips, resources, or even short video snippets. The goal is to establish authority and pique interest well before the event. Each email should include a clear call to action, encouraging recipients to register for the webinar. Offering exclusive content or bonuses for those who sign up can further increase your registration rates.

Post-webinar follow-up is equally critical. After your webinar concludes, sending a thank-you email to participants acknowledges their time and reinforces your brand's commitment to providing valuable content. This email can include a link to the recording, additional resources, or a summary of the key points discussed. Including a survey for feedback can also engage your audience and provide insights into how you can improve future webinars. This not only helps in refining your content but also fosters a sense of community among your attendees.

Incorporating automation tools can streamline your email marketing efforts, allowing you to maintain consistent communication without the need for constant manual input. By setting up automated sequences for registration confirmations, reminders, and follow-ups, you can ensure that your audience receives timely information without overwhelming yourself with repetitive tasks. This approach not only saves time but also enhances the overall experience for your audience, making them feel valued and informed.

Finally, analyzing the performance of your email campaigns is essential for ongoing improvement. Metrics such as open rates, click-through rates, and conversion rates provide invaluable data on what resonates with your audience. By conducting A/B testing on different subject lines, content formats, and sending times, you can refine your strategies to maximize engagement. Continuous learning and adaptation are crucial in the dynamic landscape of email marketing, ensuring that your content remains relevant and effective in driving participation in your webinars.

Chapter 8: Engaging Your Audience Post-Webinar

Follow-Up Strategies

Follow-up strategies are crucial in maximizing the impact of a webinar, especially when the presenter opts for a passive approach. After the webinar concludes, it is essential to maintain engagement with the audience to reinforce the message and encourage further interaction. A well-structured follow-up can turn a one-time viewer into a loyal follower or customer. This process begins with crafting a thoughtful follow-up email that acknowledges the audience's participation, summarizes the key points, and directs them to additional resources. Personalization of this email can enhance its effectiveness, creating a sense of connection and appreciation.

In addition to the initial follow-up email, consider segmenting your audience based on their engagement levels during the webinar. By analyzing metrics such as attendance duration and interaction in chat or polls, you can tailor subsequent communications to address the specific interests and needs of different audience segments. For instance, those who actively participated might appreciate more in-depth content or advanced resources, while passive viewers could benefit from introductory materials that encourage them to explore the topic further. This targeted approach fosters a deeper relationship with your audience and increases the likelihood of conversions.

Including a call to action in your follow-up communications is essential. This could range from inviting attendees to join a community, subscribe to a newsletter, or access exclusive content related to the webinar topic. By providing clear next steps, you guide your audience on how to continue their journey with your brand. Additionally, offering incentives such as discounts on products or access to a special Q&A session can motivate attendees to engage further and take advantage of your offerings.

Surveys and feedback requests are another effective follow-up strategy. Sending a brief survey to gather insights on the attendees' experience can provide valuable data for future webinars. Questions can include what they found most useful, what topics they would like to see covered next, and how they rated the overall experience. This feedback not only informs your content strategy but also shows your audience that you value their opinions and are committed to improving their experience.

Finally, consider leveraging social media platforms to extend the reach of your follow-up efforts. Sharing highlights from the webinar, posting snippets of the content, or even hosting a follow-up discussion can keep the conversation alive. Engaging with attendees on social media creates a sense of community and encourages them to share their insights with their networks. By employing a multifaceted follow-up strategy, you can maximize the long-term benefits of your webinar and cultivate a loyal audience eager for your next offering.

Gathering Feedback for Improvement

Gathering feedback is an essential component of refining your webinar content, especially for those who prefer a more passive approach to presenting. Feedback not only provides insight into the effectiveness of your material but also highlights areas that may need improvement. Utilizing surveys, polls, and follow-up emails can be effective methods to collect valuable input from your audience. By creating a structured feedback system, you can gain a clearer understanding of what resonates with your viewers and what does not.

One of the most effective ways to gather feedback is through post-webinar surveys. These surveys can be distributed immediately after the presentation, capturing the audience's reactions while the experience is still fresh in their minds. Including specific questions about content clarity, engagement, and overall satisfaction can yield actionable insights. For instance, asking participants to rate the relevance of the topics discussed can help identify which areas were most impactful and which may require more attention in future webinars.

Another useful tool for gathering feedback is the use of interactive polls during the webinar itself. These polls can engage participants in real-time, providing instant feedback on specific segments of the presentation. By asking questions related to their understanding or interest in the material being presented, you can gauge the audience's attention and adjust your content dynamically. This not only enhances engagement but also allows for immediate adjustments to improve the overall experience.

Follow-up emails serve as a valuable opportunity to reinforce your relationship with attendees while soliciting feedback. Including a brief questionnaire or a link to a more detailed survey in these emails can encourage participants to share their thoughts. Additionally, expressing gratitude for their attendance and inviting them to provide suggestions demonstrates that you value their opinions. This approach not only helps gather insights but also fosters a sense of community among your audience, making them more likely to return for future webinars.

Finally, analyzing the feedback collected is crucial for continuous improvement. Once you have gathered responses, take the time to review and categorize the data to identify trends and recurring themes. Look for common suggestions or criticisms that can guide your content development process. By implementing changes based on this feedback, you can enhance the quality of your webinars, ensuring they remain engaging and relevant to your audience's needs. This iterative process of feedback and improvement is key to mastering the lazy webinar method, ultimately leading to greater success in your passive profit endeavors.

Repurposing Webinar Content

Repurposing webinar content is a strategic approach that allows presenters to maximize the value of their efforts without the need for constant live presentations. By transforming recorded webinars into multiple forms of content, presenters can reach a wider audience and enhance their engagement levels. This process not only saves time but also ensures that quality content continues to generate leads and drive conversions long after the initial presentation has ended.

One effective method of repurposing webinar content is through the creation of bite-sized video clips. These short snippets can be shared across various social media platforms, providing teasers that entice potential viewers to watch the full webinar. By isolating key insights, tips, or moments of engagement, presenters can create compelling promotional material that highlights the value of the original content. This strategy allows for consistent engagement with the audience and encourages interaction, which can lead to increased attendance in future webinars.

Another valuable way to repurpose content is by transforming the webinar into a blog post or article. This written format allows for deeper exploration of the topics discussed during the live event. Presenters can elaborate on points made during the webinar, include additional research, or offer practical applications for the audience. This not only aids in reaching different audience segments who prefer reading over watching but also improves search engine visibility through optimized content. Including links to the original webinar recording can drive traffic back to the full presentation, creating a seamless content cycle.

Additionally, presenters can create downloadable resources such as eBooks or guides based on the content of their webinars. By compiling the key takeaways, strategies, and insights shared during the presentation, presenters can offer these valuable resources as free downloads in exchange for email subscriptions. This not only builds a mailing list for future marketing efforts but also positions the presenter as an authority in their niche. These resources can be promoted through various channels, further extending the reach of the original webinar content.

Finally, engaging with the audience through follow-up Q&A sessions can also serve as a means to repurpose webinar content. By addressing questions that arose during the initial presentation, presenters can create supplementary content that offers additional value. This can be done through a subsequent recorded session or a live-streamed event, allowing for real-time interaction. Such initiatives not only reinforce the original content but also foster a sense of community, encouraging participants to engage more deeply with future webinars and related offerings.

Chapter 9: Measuring Success

Key Metrics to Track

Key metrics play a crucial role in evaluating the effectiveness of your webinars, especially when you are not presenting live. Understanding these metrics allows you to refine your content, enhance viewer engagement, and ultimately boost conversions. The primary metrics to track include attendance rate, engagement rate, conversion rate, audience retention, and feedback scores. Each of these metrics offers valuable insights that can guide your future content strategies.

The attendance rate is a fundamental metric that reflects how many people registered for your webinar and how many actually attended. This ratio not only indicates the initial interest in your topic but also helps you gauge the effectiveness of your promotional efforts. High registration numbers with low attendance may suggest that your promotional messaging needs improvement or that the timing of the webinar does not align with your audience's availability. Tracking this metric consistently will enable you to make informed adjustments to your marketing tactics.

Engagement rate is another critical metric that measures how actively participants interacted with your webinar content. This can include actions such as clicking on links, participating in polls, or asking questions. In a pre-recorded format, you can use tools to analyze viewer interactions and determine which segments of your content resonate most with your audience. A high engagement rate indicates that your content is compelling and relevant, while a low engagement rate may signal the need for more engaging visuals, storytelling elements, or interactive components.

The conversion rate is essential for understanding the effectiveness of your webinar in driving desired actions, such as signing up for a service or purchasing a product. By tracking the number of attendees who take action after the webinar, you can assess the impact of your content and the strength of your call-to-action. If your conversion rate is lower than expected, it may be worthwhile to revisit your offer and ensure that it aligns with the needs and interests of your target audience.

Audience retention measures how long viewers stayed engaged with your webinar content. Analyzing this metric can reveal at which points viewers lost interest or dropped off entirely. This information is vital for understanding how to structure your future webinars more effectively. Maintaining a high level of audience retention often involves breaking up content into digestible segments, using storytelling techniques, and ensuring that you maintain a dynamic pace throughout the presentation. By focusing on retention, you can create a more compelling viewing experience that keeps your audience engaged from start to finish.

Lastly, feedback scores provide qualitative insights into your audience's perceptions of your webinar. Collecting feedback through surveys or polls can help you understand what viewers liked, what they found confusing, and what could be improved. This information is invaluable for refining your content, enhancing your delivery style, and ultimately crafting webinars that not only attract viewers but also convert them into loyal customers. Regularly analyzing these feedback scores in conjunction with the other key metrics will create a comprehensive picture of your webinar's performance and inform your ongoing content strategy.

Analyzing Viewer Engagement

Analyzing viewer engagement is a critical component in understanding the effectiveness of your webinar content. To gauge engagement, it is essential to examine various metrics and indicators that reveal how viewers interact with your material. Key metrics include watch time, drop-off rates, and participation in polls or Q&A sessions. By studying these elements, presenters can identify which segments of their webinars resonate most with the audience and which parts may need improvement. This analysis not only helps in refining future content but also enhances the overall viewer experience.

One of the most telling metrics is watch time, which indicates how long viewers remain engaged with the content. High watch time suggests that the material is compelling and relevant, while a significant drop-off at certain points may reveal areas that are less engaging or overly complex. Presenters should aim to keep the viewer's attention throughout the presentation, utilizing storytelling techniques, visuals, and concise information delivery. By breaking down the data, presenters can pinpoint trends and adjust their content strategy accordingly.

Drop-off rates are another vital metric that provides insight into viewer engagement. By tracking when viewers exit the webinar, presenters can identify specific moments that may cause disinterest. This could be due to lengthy explanations, lack of interactive elements, or even technical issues. Understanding these patterns allows content creators to tweak their presentations, ensuring they maintain viewer interest from start to finish. Incorporating actionable insights from drop-off analysis can lead to more engaging and effective webinars.

Participation in interactive elements, such as polls and Q&A sessions, also serves as a barometer for engagement. These features allow presenters to gauge audience interest and feedback in real time. A high level of participation indicates that viewers are actively engaged and invested in the content. In contrast, low participation may signal a need for more engaging questions or prompts. By encouraging viewer interaction, presenters can create a more dynamic atmosphere that fosters connection and keeps the audience involved throughout the presentation.

Finally, qualitative feedback should not be overlooked in the analysis of viewer engagement. Post-webinar surveys and feedback forms offer valuable insights into the audience's perceptions and experiences. This qualitative data can reveal what viewers found most beneficial, as well as areas for improvement. By synthesizing both quantitative metrics and qualitative feedback, presenters can develop a comprehensive understanding of viewer engagement, ultimately leading to the creation of more compelling and effective webinar content that resonates with their audience.

Adjusting Strategies Based on Data

Adjusting strategies based on data is essential for optimizing webinar content and ensuring it resonates with the audience. In the context of the lazy presenter, this approach shifts the focus from traditional live presentation tactics to a data-driven methodology that emphasizes the importance of pre-recorded content. By analyzing viewer engagement metrics, such as watch time, interaction rates, and drop-off points, presenters can identify which segments of their webinars captivate the audience and which fail to hold their attention. This insight allows for a targeted refinement of content, leading to more engaging and effective webinars.

One of the most critical aspects of data analysis is understanding audience behavior. Metrics collected during webinars provide valuable information about what topics generate interest and which formats are most appealing. For instance, if data reveals that viewers consistently drop off during lengthy explanations, presenters can adjust their strategies by breaking down complex information into bite-sized segments or incorporating more visual elements. This adaptability not only improves viewer retention but also enhances the overall learning experience for attendees, making it more likely that they will engage with future content.

Furthermore, feedback mechanisms play a crucial role in this adjustment process. Post-webinar surveys and polls can yield qualitative data that complements quantitative metrics. By gathering direct input from the audience, presenters gain insights into their preferences, pain points, and suggestions for improvement. This feedback loop allows for continuous refinement of content, enabling presenters to align their offerings more closely with the needs and desires of their target audience. Adjusting strategies based on this combined data sets the stage for creating webinars that are both relevant and engaging.

In addition, A/B testing can serve as a powerful tool for optimizing content based on data-driven insights. By experimenting with different formats, structures, or even topics, presenters can gather comparative data that highlights which variations resonate best with their audience. This process allows for informed decision-making, ensuring that future webinars are crafted with a clear understanding of what works. As presenters become more adept at leveraging data, they can create a feedback-rich environment that fosters innovation and continuous improvement.

Ultimately, the goal of adjusting strategies based on data is to create a seamless and enriching experience for the audience. For the lazy presenter, this means developing a robust framework that prioritizes data analysis and audience feedback. By committing to this iterative process, presenters can elevate their content, increase viewer engagement, and establish a loyal following. In a landscape where attention spans are short, adapting based on data not only sets presenters apart but also positions them for long-term success in the realm of automated webinars.

Chapter 10: Scaling Your Lazy Webinar Strategy

Creating a Webinar Series

Creating a webinar series involves strategic planning and a clear understanding of your target audience's needs and preferences. The first step is to identify a central theme that resonates with your audience. This theme should align with their interests and pain points, providing a foundation for each webinar in the series. Conducting surveys or engaging with your audience through social media can yield valuable insights into what topics will capture their attention. Once you have defined your theme, break it down into specific topics for individual webinars, ensuring each session offers unique value while contributing to the overarching theme.

Next, it is essential to outline the structure of each webinar in your series. A well-organized presentation enhances viewer engagement and retention. Start by establishing a clear objective for each session, which will guide your content creation. Create a script or outline that includes key points, anecdotes, and data to support your arguments. Additionally, consider integrating various content formats, such as slides, videos, or infographics, to cater to different learning styles. This diverse approach keeps the audience engaged and allows them to absorb information in a way that best suits them.

Another critical aspect of creating a successful webinar series is the incorporation of interactive elements. Although the focus may be on pre-recorded content, opportunities for audience interaction should not be overlooked. Utilize polls, quizzes, or Q&A segments to encourage participation and make the experience more engaging. These interactive features can help maintain viewer interest and provide valuable feedback on the content being presented. Moreover, fostering a sense of community among participants can lead to increased loyalty and repeat attendance in future webinars.

Promotion is key to the success of your webinar series. Develop a comprehensive marketing plan to reach your target audience effectively. Utilize social media platforms, email marketing, and partnerships with influencers or relevant organizations to spread the word. Create eye-catching promotional materials that highlight the benefits of attending your webinars, including learning outcomes and guest speakers, if applicable. Consistent promotion leading up to each session will help generate excitement and ensure a strong turnout, ultimately maximizing the impact of your content.

Finally, after each webinar, it is essential to gather feedback and analyze viewer engagement metrics. This data will provide insights into what worked well and what could be improved in future sessions. Consider sending out post-webinar surveys to collect participant opinions on content, pacing, and overall experience. Use this feedback to refine your approach and make adjustments to subsequent webinars in the series. By continuously evolving your content based on audience input, you can create a compelling and engaging webinar series that resonates with your audience and keeps them coming back for more.

Leveraging Partnerships and Collaborations

Leveraging partnerships and collaborations can significantly enhance the reach and effectiveness of your webinars, especially for those in the passive profit space. By identifying and engaging with complementary businesses or influencers within your niche, you can tap into their audiences and broaden your own. This approach not only increases visibility but also adds credibility to your offerings. Establishing strategic partnerships allows you to share resources, cross-promote content, and co-create engaging materials that resonate with a larger demographic.

One effective strategy for leveraging partnerships is to co-host webinars with industry experts or influencers. This not only diversifies the content but also attracts participants who may not have been familiar with your brand. Choosing partners who share a similar target audience but offer different perspectives or expertise can create a richer experience for attendees. When both parties promote the webinar through their channels, the combined marketing efforts can lead to increased attendance and engagement, ultimately boosting your passive profit potential.

Another avenue is to collaborate on content creation. This can include guest appearances on each other's webinars, joint eBooks, or shared blog posts that promote your upcoming webinars. By creating valuable resources together, both parties benefit from each other's knowledge and exposure. This collaborative content can serve as a powerful tool for building your email list, as participants are often willing to exchange their information for high-quality resources. Moreover, the endorsement from a respected partner enhances your credibility and can lead to higher conversion rates.

It's also important to engage in affiliate marketing partnerships. By offering affiliates a commission for promoting your webinar, you incentivize them to share your content with their audiences. This creates a win-win scenario where the affiliate earns revenue while you gain access to a broader audience. Ensure that your affiliate partners are well-aligned with your brand values and messaging to maintain authenticity and trust with potential attendees. This approach not only drives registrations but can also lead to long-term relationships that sustain your passive income stream.

Lastly, regularly assess and refine your partnership strategies. Keep track of which collaborations yield the best results in terms of attendance, engagement, and conversions. Solicit feedback from partners and participants to understand what worked and what could be improved. By continually optimizing your partnerships, you can enhance your webinar strategy, ensuring that your content remains engaging and relevant while reducing the workload typically associated with live presentations. Emphasizing collaboration allows you to leverage the strengths of others, ultimately leading to a more impactful and efficient webinar experience.

Expanding Your Reach and Influence

Expanding your reach and influence is essential for maximizing the potential of your webinars, particularly when employing the lazy presenter method. This approach allows you to pre-record your content, enabling you to focus on quality and engagement without the pressure of live performance. To effectively broaden your audience, it's crucial to leverage various platforms and strategies that align with your target market. Social media channels, email newsletters, and collaborations with influencers in your niche can significantly enhance visibility and attract more participants to your webinars.

Utilizing social media for promotion offers a vast array of opportunities. Platforms like Facebook, Instagram, LinkedIn, and Twitter allow you to share snippets of your webinar content, behind-the-scenes glimpses, or testimonials from previous attendees. Engaging with your audience through polls, questions, and discussions can also foster a community feeling, making your webinars more appealing. Creating shareable graphics or short video teasers can generate buzz and encourage your followers to spread the word, thus increasing your reach exponentially.

Email marketing remains one of the most effective means of communication for nurturing relationships with your audience. Building an email list allows you to segment your audience based on interests and tailor your messages accordingly. Crafting compelling subject lines and providing valuable content in your newsletters can pique interest and drive attendance to your webinars. Additionally, follow-up emails post-webinar can maintain engagement, offer further resources, and solicit feedback, ensuring your audience feels valued and more likely to return for future sessions.

Collaborating with influencers and thought leaders in your niche can serve as a catalyst for expanding your influence. Partnering with individuals who share a similar audience can introduce your content to new viewers who are already interested in your topics. Co-hosting webinars or offering guest appearances can provide mutual benefits, allowing both parties to leverage each other's platforms. This not only increases your reach but also enhances your credibility, as potential attendees often trust recommendations from familiar figures in their field.

Lastly, optimizing your content for search engines can significantly enhance your visibility. Utilizing keywords relevant to your niche within your webinar descriptions, titles, and promotional materials can help your content rank higher in search results. Additionally, consider repurposing your webinar content into blog posts, podcasts, or social media snippets to attract different audience segments. By diversifying your content and utilizing SEO best practices, you can ensure that your webinars reach a wider audience, ultimately increasing your influence and establishing you as a thought leader in your field.